The Church and Divorce

by A. R. WINNETT Ph.D.

Vicar of Grayshott, Honorary Canon of Guildford Cathedral and Examining Chapter to the Bishop of Guildford

THIS BOOK sets out to provide an exact and comprehensive survey of the whole question of divorce and the related problem of the re-marriage of divorced persons; and of the changes and developments in the Church's practice through the years. Canon Winnett, who is an acknowledged expert in this field, begins with a historical retrospect of the Church of England's position in this matter, and passes on to recent Anglican developments. He then looks at churches of the Anglican Communion overseas and makes plain their own varying attitudes, with particular reference to the new canons of the Church in Canada. After that, he considers the same questions in an ecumenical context, as they affect other churches. The recent report, *Putting Asunder*, is then considered and explained, and he concludes with a thought-provoking chapter on 'A Marriage Discipline for the Future.'

Canon Winnett himself has been married for twenty-five years, and is the father of two daughters, aged twenty-one and nineteen.

Mowbrays

SBN 264 65566 4

10s. 6d. net

The Church and Divorce

A FACTUAL SURVEY

A. R. Winnett

Mowbrays

THE CHURCH AND DIVORCE

By the same author
Divorce and Remarriage in Anglicanism (Macmillan)

The Church and Divorce

by

A. R. WINNETT, Ph.D.

Vicar of Grayshott,
Honorary Canon of Guildford Cathedral and
Examining Chaplain to the Bishop of Guildford

LONDON
A. R. MOWBRAY & CO LTD

Printed in Great Britain by
Alden & Mowbray Ltd
at the Alden Press, Oxford

SBN 264 65566 4

First published in 1968

To
Geraldine and Bridget

CONTENTS

ACKNOWLEDGEMENTS

The thanks of the author and publishers are due to the following for permission to quote from books:

Constable Publishers, *No New Morality* by D. A. Rhymes; Faith Press Ltd., *Law and Love* by Helen Oppenheimer; Victor Gollancz Ltd., *Common Sense About Sexual Ethics* by D. S. Bailey; Hodder & Stoughton Ltd., *Christian Ethics and Secular Society* by F. R. Barry and *Marriage and Divorce* by K. E. Kirk; Methuen & Co. Ltd., *Marriage Was Made for Man* by A. P. Shepherd; Laurence Pollinger Ltd., *A Time for Christian Candour* by J. A. Pike; S.C.M. Press Ltd., *Morals in a Free Society* by Michael Keeling, *Essays in Anglican Self-Criticism* edited by D. M. Paton, *Honest to God* and *Christian Morals Today* by J. A. T. Robinson, *Men and Women* by G. Russell, and *A New Introduction to Moral Theology* by H. M. Waddams; S.P.C.K., *Marriage* by W. Boulton; *Problems of Marriage and Divorce* by G. F. Fisher, *Marriage in Church and State* by T. A. Lacey and R. C. Mortimer, *Remarriage and Mixed Marriage* by H. W. Montefiore, *How the Church of England Works* by P. A. Welsby and *The Church and the Law of Nullity of Marriage.*

Thanks are also due to the following for permission to quote extracts:

The Anglican Church of Canada, *Canon XXVII On Marriage in the Church;* Church Assembly Board of Social Responsibility, *The Marriage Covenant;* The Church of Scotland General Assembly, *Act of the Marriage of Divorced Persons;* the Editor of *Clergy Review,* article, 'Vatican II and Marriage' by J. Dominian; Faculty Office of the Archbishop of Canterbury and S.P.C.K., *Putting Asunder;* Her Majesty's Stationery Office, *Royal Commission on Marriage and Divorce, Cmnd. 9678* and the *Divorce Reform Bill, 1968;* Her Majesty's Stationery Office and the Law Commission, *Reform of the Grounds of Divorce: the Field of Choice, Cmnd. 3123;* the Right Hon. Lord Denning, Master of the Rolls, *The Divorce Laws.*

PREFACE

This book is primarily intended as a survey of the teaching and practice of the Church of England and the other Churches of the Anglican Communion, and the Roman Catholic, Orthodox and Reformed Churches, in the matter of divorce and remarriage. The growing ecumenical dialogue at the present time and the various reunion schemes now under discussion make it necessary to treat the subject in a context wider than a purely Anglican one. As a survey this book may be regarded as a continuation and extension of my earlier volume, *Divorce and Remarriage in Anglicanism,* published in 1958.

It is, however, hardly possible for an author to treat so controversial a subject as divorce and remarriage without giving some indication of his own views, and I have not sought to conceal mine. Here I have to acknowledge that what I have now written represents a departure from the standpoint which I adopted ten years ago in the work above mentioned. I have come to attribute greater importance to the actual personal relationship in marriage as distinct from a bond or *vinculum* believed to exist independently of this relationship, and this in turn reflects the development of my theological thinking in the direction of rediscovering what H. H. Farmer has termed the 'radical personalism' of the Christian Gospel.

Though I have in my pastoral practice always observed the Resolutions of Convocation out of loyalty both to episcopal direction and to the mind of the Church as expressed in those Resolutions I have come increasingly to question the basis on which they rest, and to feel that the time has come for a reconsideration of the Church's position in respect of divorce and remarriage. I believe this view to be shared by a large number of churchpeople, both clergy and laity. Nevertheless as a survey of existing teaching and practice in the various branches of the Christian Church the ensuing study will, I trust, possess a usefulness unaffected by the personal opinions of the author.

I would here express my gratitude to those who have kindly answered my enquiries and supplied me with information: the Archbishops of Wales, Dublin, West Africa, East Africa, Uganda, Central Africa, Melbourne, Brisbane, Perth, New Zealand, and the West Indies; the Bishop Primus of the Episcopal Church in Scotland, the Archbishop in Jerusalem, and the Metropolitan of the Church in India, Pakistan, Burma and Ceylon; the Bishops of Adelaide, Tasmania, Willochra, New York, Saskatoon and Huron; the Roman Catholic

Bishop of Portsmouth; the Registrar of the Diocese of Sydney; the Senior Chaplain to the Archbishop of Capetown; the Secretary of the Law Commission; the Rev. Professor J. C. Blackie, of the University of Edinburgh; the Rev. Professor J. M. Barkley, of the Assembly's College, Belfast; Professor Stuart Ryan, of Queen's University, Kingston, Ontario; the Secretary of the Advisory Group on Sex, Marriage and the Family of the British Council of Churches; the General Secretary of the Presbyterian Church of England; the Secretary of the Presbyterian Church of Wales; the Secretary of the Methodist Department of Christian Citizenship; and the Secretary of the Citizenship Committee of the Baptist Union.

Grayshott Vicarage,
Hindhead.
March, 1968.

A. R. WINNETT

INTRODUCTION

A mother was telling her five-year old daughter about her numerous relations and who was married to whom. At the end of the recital the child asked, 'And haven't any of them been divorced?' This might be cited as evidence of what is sometimes called 'divorce-mindedness',[1] that is, the acceptance of divorce as a normal procedure for dealing with a marriage that has 'failed to work'. Judges and other eminent persons have animadverted upon this attitude to divorce. Lord Denning, now Master of the Rolls, said in 1947:

> 'Some young people approach marriage with the feeling that if it does not work out well they can always get a divorce. If that goes on, we shall be approaching the stage of universal trial marriage. It is a serious state of affairs.'[2]

Shortly afterwards a priest-psychiatrist was writing:

> 'A couple who face the problems of married life are aware that a host of others who failed to solve them got out of them, by divorce; and the knowledge adds to their task. Their energies and their emotions are less than fully engaged. They do not "need" to succeed; and success is therefore more difficult. And the vicious spiral goes on.'[3]

Undoubtedly there is a measure of truth in this gloomy diagnosis, but it may easily be exaggerated. It is necessary first of all to look at the figures. At the beginning of the present century in England and Wales some 800 petitions for divorce were filed annually; by 1914 it had risen to about 1000; and in the years 1936-40 the annual average reached 7500, the increase being partly due to the new grounds of divorce introduced by the Herbert Act of 1937.[4] The peak year was 1947 when 48,501 petitions were filed, and 60,254 decrees absolute granted, the latter high figure reflecting the success of the Courts in dealing with arrears of work. Thereafter the figures began to fall until in 1958 26,239 petitions were presented and 22,654 decrees abso-

1. It should in honesty be mentioned that the child's father was at the time engaged in writing a book on divorce, so the subject must often have been talked about in her hearing.
2. *The Divorce Laws* (lecture at King's College, London), p. 31.
3. Gilbert Russell, *Men and Women*, p. 59.
4. O. R. McGregor, *Divorce in England*, p. 36.

lute granted.[5] A steady rise has taken place since 1959, and in 1966 46,609 petitions were filed and 39,067 decrees absolute granted.[6]

Before concluding that these figures indicate a general breakdown of marriage or a collapse in moral standards we must bear in mind that an increase in the number of divorces does not necessarily mean more broken homes: it may only mean that more cases of marriage breakdown now end in divorce. Whereas at one time many couples parted only to enter into new and irregular unions, today as the result of enlarged grounds of divorce and the availability of legal aid,[7] recourse is had to the Courts for a dissolution. Social factors also enter in, such as the greater degree to which wives are now economically independent of their husbands. The increase in the number of divorces must be viewed in the light of the increase in population, the tendency to marry younger, and the longer expectation of life, factors which mean both that there are more marriages and that marriages are at risk for longer than formerly. The married population and the average duration of marriage have approximately doubled during the present century. The divorce rate per 1000 married couples was in 1955 2.4; in 1960 2.0; and in 1964 2.9.[8] In 1952 Professor R. M. Titmuss could reach the following admittedly tentative conclusion:

> 'It is probable that the proportion of broken marriages under the age of sixty, marriages broken by death, desertion and divorce is, in total, smaller today than at any time this century despite the rise in the number of divorces.'[9]

Though statistics do not support the idea of an alarming deterioration in matrimonial stability, they nevertheless reveal a situation which cannot be viewed with equanimity. Every broken marriage represents a tragic breakdown in human relationship, entailing suffering to the parties and perhaps even more to the children involved. There is little evidence to determine whether greater harm is done to

5. The Law Commission, *Reform of the Grounds of Divorce: The Field of Choice* (1966), Appendix D. Petitions for nullity are included in these figures, but the number is relatively small.
6. *The Times*, 16th January, 1968. Included in the totals given are 999 nullity petitions and 715 nullity decrees.
7. In 1965 70 per cent of petitioners were legally aided.
8. Law Commission, *Reform of the Grounds of Divorce*, pp. 6-9; G. R. Dunstan, *The Family is not Broken*, pp. 66-70.
9. Quoted in Dunstan, op.cit., p. 70.

children by the divorce of parents or by the quarrels of parents living together, but either way the children suffer.

The Church must inevitably be deeply concerned with marriage and with the problem of marriage breakdown, for whatever uncertainty may surround the detailed application of Christ's teaching on marriage, there is no doubt that for him marriage was part of the natural order ordained by God and its lifelong character grounded in the plan and purpose of God 'from the beginning'.[10] From the earliest times, as is evident from the New Testament,[11] some form of marriage discipline has existed in the Church, prescribing conditions for the recognition or the solemnization of marriages and the action to be taken when those who are married repudiate the obligations of marriage. But the Church's concern for marriage must extend beyond its own members for the very reason that marriage is part of the natural order, and the Church cannot dissociate itself from the world which God created and which Christ has redeemed. The Church must therefore strive for the health and stability of marriage in society as a whole, though it will not seek to impose upon an only partially Christian society a doctrine and law of marriage identical with its own. An Established Church, like the Church of England, has, as the authors of *Putting Asunder* point out, a special responsibility to the society in the midst of which it is set.[12]

By its teaching and discipline the Church has sought, in differing ways and with varying degrees of success, to bear witness to the Christian conception of marriage, but a significant development in modern times is the Church's active endeavour to ensure that as many marriages as possible fulfil the Christian ideal of what marriage is meant to be. The care now taken by the majority of clergy and ministers in preparing couples for marriage, the friendship and counsel given by Church Social Workers, and the fine work done by Marriage Guidance Counsellors, many of whom are committed Christians and churchmen, in cases of threatened marriage breakdown, are practical ways in which the Church seeks to promote happy and stable marriage and to reduce the toll of divorce. The fact that this book is so largely concerned with the undoing of marriage, or divorce, and with the Church's attitude to divorce, makes it all the more necessary to call attention here to the positive and constructive aspect of the Church's concern for marriage, and to pay tribute to whom tribute is due.

10. Mark 10. 6. 11. e.g. I Corinthians 7. 12. *Putting Asunder*, p. 13.

I.

THE CHURCH OF ENGLAND AND DIVORCE: A HISTORICAL RETROSPECT

The Continental Reformers, in their opposition to the complexities of Canon Law and to a system which (to quote Canon Lacey) 'failed miserably as guardian of the holy estate',[1] swept away the whole mediaeval catalogue of impediments to marriage other than those which they believed to have scriptural sanction. A marriage was no longer to be ended on the ground of some canonical flaw, but in general they were agreed that divorce, in the sense of a dissolution of the marriage-bond, should be allowed for adultery and malicious desertion. Divorce for adultery was held to be permitted by our Lord's teaching recorded by St. Matthew, while divorce for malicious desertion was justified by reference to I Corinthians 7. 15 and I Timothy 5. 8, the deserter being on a par with a heathen or unbeliever.[2] A few, such as Martin Bucer, were prepared to allow divorce for a wider range of causes.[3] The Anglican Reformers for the most part adopted the views of their more moderate Continental brethren, though Cranmer did so only after considerable hesitation and weighing of the scriptural and patristic evidence, as his *Collectiones de Divortio* in Lambeth Palace Library bear witness.[4] The proposed code of Canons known as the *Reformatio Legum Ecclesiasticarum*, had it passed into law, would have brought the practice of the Church of England into line with that advocated by the more advanced Continental Reformers, who largely influenced its production. In it, adultery, desertion, deadly hostility and prolonged ill-treatment of a wife by a husband were admitted as grounds of divorce. The *Reformatio Legum* had not been enacted when Edward VI died, and an attempt to revive it under Elizabeth I proved abortive.[5]

1. Lacey-Mortimer, *Marriage in Church and State,* p. 137.
2. Luther, *The Babylonian Captivity,* in *Works* (Philadelphia edition) II., p. 272.
3. For Bucer not only adultery and desertion but also serious crime, impotence, leprosy and insanity were just grounds of divorce. John Milton translated the section on Divorce from Bucer's *De Regno Christi* under the title *The Judgment of Martin Bucer concerning Divorce,* (1644).
4. On the *Collectiones* see Dibdin and Chadwyck-Healey, *English Church Law and Divorce,* Appendix E, and Winnett, *Divorce and Remarriage in Anglicanism,* pp. 56-59.
5. Winnett, op. cit., pp. 26-34; Appendix by Dr. Sherwin Bailey on the *Reformatio Legum* in *The Church and Marriage* (second edition 1954).

The views concerning divorce and remarriage current at the time of the Reformation did not find a corresponding expression in the practice of the Church of England. As Sir Lewis Dibdin conclusively showed, the Church Courts continued to grant only decrees of nullity and separation (divorce *a mensa et thoro*), and the Visitation Articles of the bishops coupled remarriage after divorce with other matrimonial offences such as bigamy. The second marriage of the Earl of Northampton in 1547, his former wife having been divorced for adultery, required a special Act of Parliament to render it lawful, and the Act specifically claimed to override the existing ecclesiastical law.[6] The Canons of 1597 relating to marriage, incorporated in the Canons of 1604, provided only for the 'annulling of pretended matrimony' and for divorce *a mensa et thoro,* in the latter case the parties being required to enter into a bond not to remarry during the other's lifetime.[7] There is evidence that a certain number of second marriages after divorce did take place in the latter half of the sixteenth century and later, and in view of the opinion held by many churchmen that adultery dissolved the marriage-bond and that at least the innocent party was free to remarry, their occurrence is not to be wondered at. They were, however, exceptional and irregular, and did not reflect the official practice of the Church of England.[8]

During the seventeenth century Anglican divines were divided in their views as to the lawfulness of divorce *a vinculo.* Some, like Edmund Bunny, Bishop Andrewes, John Howson and Thomas Comber, held marriage to be indissoluble absolutely.[9] Others maintained that the teaching of Christ allowed divorce *a vinculo* for the one cause of adultery, with the right of remarriage for the innocent party. Of this position John Rainolds, Henry Hammond, Bishop Joseph Hall and

6. Dibdin and Chadwyck-Healey, op.cit., pp. 62-69; Winnett, op.cit., pp. 40-42.
7. Canon 107.
8. In 1572 Archbishop Parker granted a licence for the marriage of Sir John Stawell to Frances Dyer, his former wife having been divorced for adultery. Edmund Bunny, *Of Divorce for Adultery and Marrying Again,* (1596), and Lancelot Andrewes, *Against Second Marriage After Sentence of Divorce,* (1601), both refer to second marriages after divorce as having taken place at the time at which they wrote. The Bigamy Act of 1603 exempted from the penalties of the Act those who remarried after a decree of separation granted by the Ecclesiastical Court.
9. Bunny, *Of Divorce for Adultery and Marrying Again*; Andrewes, *Against Second Marriage after Sentence of Divorce;* Howson, *Uxore Dimissa propter fornicationem aliam non licet superinducere,* (1606); Comber, *A Companion to the Temple,* (1678).

Herbert Thorndike may be taken as representatives.[10] Andrew Willet, just before the beginning of the century, and Bishop John Cosin were alone in holding desertion as well as adultery to be a ground of divorce *a vinculo.* [11]

The difficulty of the question as it presented itself to an able and resolute mind of the seventeenth century is shown by the wavering attitude of William Laud, who appears more than once to have undergone a change of opinion on the matter of divorce.[12]

The Ecclesiastical Courts granting only divorce *a mensa et thoro,* the only way a divorce *a vinculo* could be obtained was by private Act of Parliament. In 1670 a Bill was introduced to enable Lord Roos to remarry during the lifetime of his wife, against whom the Ecclesiastical Court had granted a decree of divorce *a mensa et thoro* on the ground of her adultery. The Bill met with considerable opposition, largely for political reasons,[13] but Cosin was one of its main supporters, his speeches in the Lords being published as a pamphlet, *Argument proving that Adultery works a Dissolution of the Marriage.* For Cosin the reality of marriage consists in the personal relationship of husband and wife: it is separation from bed and board, and not merely the remarriage, which is a breach of the marriage-bond, and

10. Rainolds, *Defence of the Judgment of the Reformed Churches that a Man may lawfully not only put away his Wife for her Adultery, but also marry Another,* (1609); Hammond, *Practical Catechism* Book II, (1644), and *Letter of Resolution to Six Queries of Present Use in the Church of England,* (1653); Hall, *Resolutions and Decisions of Divers Practical Cases of Conscience,* (1649); Thorndike, *Epilogue to the Tragedy of the Church of England,* Book II, (1659). Thorndike holds that though the innocent party may by God's law remarry, yet the Church of England is within its rights in restricting this liberty.

11. Willet, *Synopsis Papismi,* 3rd edition, (1600); Cosin, *Argument proving that Adultery works a Dissolution of the Marriage,* (1670). The marriage-vow, says Cosin, does not extend to 'tolerating adultery, or malicious desertion, which according to God's ordinance, dissolves the marriage'. Cosin, *Works,* (Library of Anglo-Catholic Theology) IV, p. 493.

12. In 1605 Laud married Charles Blount, Earl of Devonshire, to Lady Penelope Rich, divorced by her husband for adultery with the Earl, though Laud afterwards repented of having performed the marriage. The Earl wrote a tract defending his second marriage, and Laud replied in his *Censure of the Earl of Devonshire's Tract touching Marriage and Divorce,* in which he upholds the indissolubilist position. Yet Laud's copy of Bellarmine in Marsh's Library, Dublin, contains notes in his handwriting controverting the indissolubilist view. Laud's Scottish Canons of 1636 provide only for divorce *a mensa et thoro* with an express caution against remarriage. Winnett, op. cit. Ch. VI.

13. The King saw in the Bill a possible precedent for divorcing his childless queen and taking a new partner, a course to which he was being urged by Buckingham. The opposition to the Bill was led by the Duke of York, whose succession to the throne would be frustrated if a legitimate child were born to the King. For a full account of the Roos case and Cosin's part in it, see Winnett, op. cit., Ch. VII.

the distinction between the marriage-bond and the actual sharing of bed and board is 'merely chimerical and fancy'.[14] Nevertheless the innocent party may lawfully marry again, and Cosin argues at length in support of this from scripture, the Fathers and the Reformed divines. The Bill was given a third reading in the Lords by a majority of seven votes, and in November 1671 Lord Roos married Diana, widow of Sir Seymour Shirley. The Archbishop of York and thirteen other bishops voted against the third reading. The authority attaching to Cosin's name was doubtless influential in overcoming the hesitations which many churchmen felt regarding remarriage after divorce, and to others the attitude of Cosin, as a High Churchman, has been a cause of perplexity.[15] But the line taken by Cosin on divorce and remarriage was that taken by a number of Anglican divines of the period, and one for which it was believed there was clear scriptural authority.

The action of Parliament in the Roos case afforded a precedent which was followed with increasing frequency until the passing of the Divorce Act in 1857. Over a period of 187 years, 317 private Acts were passed, with little if any opposition from the Church as represented by the bishops in the House of Lords, through the bishops supported the efforts which were made from time to time to prevent the marriage of a guilty party to his or her partner in guilt. A number of instances of second marriages after the first marriage has been dissolved by Act of Parliament are found in the parish registers of the period.[16]

The eighteenth century, with its emphasis on reason and natural law and its tendency to Erastian views of Church and State, saw the almost complete disappearance of the indissolubilist view from the Church of England.[17] Bishop Fleetwood takes it for granted that a

14. Cosin, *Works* (L.A.C.T.), IV, p. 492. Earlier Bishop Hall had described the notion of a bond apart from the duties of bed and board as 'merely chimerical, nothing but fantasy'. *Works*, VII, p. 378.

15. Cosin's strong anti-Romanism may have been a factor, especially as the Duke of York had embraced the Roman Catholic faith. Keble regarded Cosin as typical of those 'who lay hold of every topic for disparaging and counteracting the Church of Rome, without always taking pains to enquire whether the very true Church of the Father was not being pierced through her side'. *Sequel to the Argument against immediately repealing the Laws which treat the Nuptial Bond as indissoluble,* p. 241.

16. Winnett, op. cit., pp. 128-130.

17. By way of supplementing the paragraph on Thomas Wilson, Bishop of Sodor and Man, on p. 99 of my *Divorce and Remarriage in Anglicanism* I may mention that Wilson granted a licence to remarry to a man whose wife had been sentenced to death for sheep-stealing, the sentence being commuted to seven years' transportation on condition that she did not return to the island without the Governor's permission. The husband was left with children, 'one still at the breast'.

marriage may be dissolved for adultery, and he denounces those who deny the innocent party the right of remarriage as unwilling to 'use the reason and good sense which God has given them'.[18] Paley at the end of the century argues for the permanence of marriage from natural law, which requires that children should not be deprived of maternal care, and from considerations of social expediency. Though the natural law would admit of exceptions in the case of adultery, desertion, insanity and attempted murder, yet 'scripture seems to have drawn the obligation tighter than the law of nature left it', and for Paley Christ's word is decisive in limiting the permission of divorce to the one case of the wife's adultery.[19]

The 1857 Matrimonial Causes Act, which was to set up a special civil court empowered to dissolve marriages *a vinculo* on the ground of a wife's adultery, or a husband's adultery if there were aggravating circumstances,[20] met with a varying reception on the part of churchmen and revealed the difference of opinion which existed concerning divorce and remarriage. Of all the bishops, Tait of London gave it the strongest support in the Lords: in his opinion it would mean no change in what had been the Church's practice during the previous hundred years or more, and it had the merit of substituting a regular court procedure for the haphazard method of private Bills. A small group of bishops, led by Wilberforce of Oxford and Kerr Hamilton of Salisbury, opposed the Bill on the ground that marriage by our Lord's teaching admitted of no dissolution. The majority of the bishops, however, supported the Bill, but with some reluctance, which was due not to their holding marriage to be indissoluble, but to the liberty of remarriage which the Bill gave to the guilty party. A clause was embodied in the final form of the Act permitting an incumbent to refuse to solemnise the marriage of a guilty divorced person, but compelling him to allow the use of his church if another clergyman were willing to officiate.[21]

At the time the Divorce Bill was introduced the Tractarian or Ox-

18. *The Counsellor's Plea for the Divorce of Sir G. D. and Mrs. F.*, in *Works*, III, p. 335.
19. *Moral and Political Philosophy*, Book III, part iii, ch. 7.
20. In 1923 simple adultery on the part of a husband was made a ground of divorce.
21. Winnett, op. cit., Ch. IX.

The bishop held that remarriage in this case did not contravene either "the rules of our holy Religion or the orders and determination of learned and judicious Christians in all ages". *Works*, edited by Keble (L. A.C.T.), I, p. 107. (I am grateful to Professor Gordon Dunstan for this reference.)

ford Movement had become an influential force in the Church, and John Keble, one of the leading Tractarians, opposed the Bill in two pamphlets, *An Argument for not proceeding immediately to repeal the Laws which treat the Nuptial Bond as indissoluble* and *Sequel of the Argument against immediately repealing the Laws which treat the Nuptial Bond as indissoluble.* Keble was among the first to realise that marriage meant two different things for the Church and for a state which was becoming increasingly secular. Parliament might make what marriage-laws it would for those who were not churchmen, but 'neither is Parliament free to ordain, nor the Church to obey, anything which affects Holy Matrimony as it is a spiritual and supernatural ordinance'. Keble draws a distinction between marriages which are 'blessed in heaven' and those that are merely 'agreed on earth', and it is only the former which he believes to possess the character of indissolubility.[22]

A churchman who welcomed the 1857 Act was F. D. Maurice, who in a sermon preached in Lincoln's Inn Chapel saw in the disappearance of the Church's jurisdiction over marriage the liberation of the Church from a legalism which was alien to Christ's teaching on marriage.

> 'If we suppose our Lord', he said, 'in this text, Matthew 5. 32, or any other to have set aside the Mosaic code and to have substituted a new code of Christendom, we empty the words of all their life, of all the power they have exercised over mankind. For those words - those few simple words - have exercised a mighty power over mankind, just because they are not corrective of an outward policy, but belong to that internal regeneration which the Son of man came to effect for the world.'[23]

Maurice held that marriage might rightly be dissolved for adultery, but this being so it was better that the dissolution should be effected by a secular court which would be governed by the ordinary maxims of English justice and not by the subtleties of Canon Law.[24]

It would be true to say that at the time of the Divorce Act of 1857 and until the end of the century the majority of churchmen held that divorce was allowable within the limits of the Matthaean Exception, with the right of remarriage for the innocent party. This was apparently the view of the great Tractarian, E. B. Pusey,[25] and it was

22. *Sequel etc.,* p. 217   23. *Lincoln's Inn Sermons,* II, p. 310.
24. Ibid., p. 319.
25. This is implied in a letter to Pusey from Gladstone, who refers to Pusey's disagreement with Keble on the remarriage of the innocent party. *Letters on Church and State* (edited by D. C. Lathbury), I, pp. 136-7.

certainly the view of such convinced High Churchmen as Bishop Christopher Wordsworth,[26] William Bright,[27] and Bishop Edward King.[28]

Mandell Creighton, a great and wise bishop, first of Peterborough and later of London, as well as a distinguished scholar and historian, gave his judgment on the matter in the following words, written in 1895:

> 'We must remember - it cannot be remembered too much - that the Gospel consists of principles not of maxims. The only possible principle concerning marriage is that it is indissoluble. But all principles are set aside by sin, and our Lord recognised that as regards marriage . . . We as Christians abhor divorce, but when a divorce has been judged necessary are we to refuse any liberty to the innocent and wronged party? It seems to me a matter for our discretion on equitable grounds in each case. I could not advise any of my clergy to refuse to solemnise a marriage of an innocent person who genuinely desired God's blessing. I prefer to err on the side of charity.'[29]

At the beginning of the present century a significant change occurred in Anglican opinion on divorce and remarriage, and took the form of a strengthening of the indissolubilist position. Many factors contributed to this. New Testament criticism questioned the Exceptive Clause in St. Matthew (not found in St. Mark) as an authentic word of Jesus. The Anglo-Catholic movement, with a moral theology largely derived from Roman sources, had gained ground among the clergy. Divorce, moreover, was no longer an exceptional occurrence, but had come to be regarded as a major challenge to the Christian conception of marriage demanding an uncompromising stand on the part of the Church.[30]

An illustration of the change was provided by the 1908 Lambeth Conference, which not only reaffirmed the resolution of the 1888

26. *Occasional Sermons,* Series VI, preface to Sermon L; *Miscellanies* III, pp. 202-3.
27. *Selected Letters of William Bright,* (edited by B. J. Kidd), pp. 9-11.
28. G. W. E. Russell, *Edward King,* p. 280.
29. L. Creighton, *Life and Letters of Mandell Creighton,* II, pp. 68-69. At the same time Creighton seems to have recognised the difficulty of using the Prayer Book service in the case of marriage after divorce. Ibid. p. 275.
30. The reasons for the Church's move towards a stricter marriage discipline in the early years of the present century are outlined by Archbishop Fisher, *Problems of Marriage and Divorce,* p. 18.

Conference that the remarriage of a guilty party should not receive the blessing of the Church, but also declared it undesirable that the remarriage of an innocent party should receive the blessing of the Church.[31] A further illustration of the change is afforded by a comparison of Bishop Gore's book *The Question of Divorce* (1911) with his earlier work, *The Sermon on the Mount* (1895).[32]

The questioning of the authenticity of the Matthaean Exception had a further consequence, in that those who took the non-indissolubilist view of marriage came to base their case less on a particular version of our Lord's words than on the more general consideration that our Lord in his teaching on marriage was giving not a law, but an ideal or principle, the translation of which into practice necessitated allowance for 'hard cases' and for human sin and frailty. This was clearly apparent in the evidence given before the 1909 Royal Commission on Divorce and Matrimonial Causes by such prominent Liberal Church men as Dr. W. R. Inge, Dr. Hastings Rashdall and Dr. Hensley Henson, all of whom were prepared to regard other grounds of divorce besides adultery, for example cruelty, insanity and habitual drunkenness, as acceptable to the Christian conscience.[33]

The Lambeth Conference of 1920 in its resolution on marriage affirmed as 'our Lord's principle and standard of marriage a lifelong and indissoluble union', this being the first occasion when in such a resolution the word 'indissoluble' was used. It did, however, admit the right of a national or regional Church to make its own rules in respect of cases falling within the scope of the Matthaean Exception. The 1930 Lambeth Conference went further and recommended that no marriage of a divorced person with a partner living should be celebrated with the rites of the Church, and that where an innocent party had remarried and desired to receive Holy Communion, the case should be referred to the bishop for consideration. The Lambeth Resolution (No. 11) of 1930 laid down the lines which all subsequent actionwas to follow, and it formed the basis of the resolutions which were brought before the Convocations as the result of the Report of the Joint Committees of the Convocations in 1935.

In 1932 the Joint Committees on Marriage of the Convocations of Canterbury and York began their sessions under the chairmanship of

31. For the resolutions of the Lambeth Conferences see the appendix on pages 14-17.

32. *The Sermon on the Mount,* p. 75; *The Question of Divorce,* pp. 23-27; G. L. Prestige, *Life of Charles Gore,* pp. 126-7.

33. Winnett, op. cit. pp. 197-8.

the Bishops of Salisbury (Donaldson) and Sheffield (Burrows), and their Report was issued three years later. The Majority Report affirmed unequivocally the principle of indissolubility: marriage 'not only ought not to be dissolved but also involves a moral and spiritual bond which cannot be finally terminated save by death'.[34] Where a second marriage after divorce had taken place and one or both of the parties desired to receive Holy Communion, the case was to be referred to the bishop, 'who will consider all the circumstances of the particular case, including the questions whether the parties have acted in all good conscience and after mature reflection, and whether the abiding together as man and wife is morally preferable to any other course'.[35] The Minority Report, signed among others by Dr. Barnes, Bishop of Birmingham, declared that the indissolubility of marriage was not a law but an ideal, and that 'the mind of Christ would approve of legislation on the part of his Church which, while keeping ever in view the divine ideal, had compassionate consideration for the troubles arising from failures to live up to that ideal, and might be changed from time to time to meet the requirements of changing conditions'. The Minority Report recommended that, while the Church should be free to forbid the use of its buildings for the marriages of divorced persons, it should accord generous treatment to an undoubtedly innocent party.[36]

After prolonged discussion of the Joint Committees' Report both Convocations passed resolutions in June, 1938, to the effect that marriage is 'a personal union, for better or for worse, of one man with one woman, exclusive of all others on either side, and indissoluble save by death'; that 'remarriage after divorce during the lifetime of a former partner always involves a departure from the true principle of marriage as declared by our Lord'; and that 'in order to maintain the principle of lifelong obligation which is inherent in every legally contracted marriage and is expressed in plainest terms in the Marriage Service, the Church should not allow the use of that Service in the case of anyone who has a former partner living'. On the question of the admission of divorced persons to Communion the Upper House of Canterbury resolved that they might be admitted by the bishop, provided he were satisfied that they were conscientiously persuaded that it was right for them to live together as man and wife, and that their admission would be for the good of their souls and

34. Report of the Joint Committees, *The Church and Marriage,* p. 18.
35. Ibid., p. 25. 36. Ibid., pp. 34-38.

would not be a cause of scandal to the Church. The York Convocation adopted a resolution concerning admission to Communion on the lines of that contained in the Majority Report, but the Lower House of Canterbury, in view of the division of opinion in the House, postponed consideration of the question indefinitely. The bishops, however, declared that they would act upon the resolution of the Upper House in the exercise of their pastoral responsibility.[37]

The freedom of the clergy in law to act upon the resolutions of the Convocations in the matter of the remarriage of divorced persons was the result of the Matrimonial Causes Act of 1937 (the 'Herbert Act'). This Act, which extended the grounds of divorce to include desertion, cruelty and incurable insanity, also contained a clause providing that no clergyman should be compelled to solemnize the marriage of any divorced person whose former partner was still living, or to permit his church to be used for such a marriage.[38] Though the Act of 1937 left the clergy free to solemnize or not to solemnize the marriages of divorced persons, and though strictly the Convocation resolutions had only the force of recommendations or strong expressions of opinion,[39] most of the bishops directed their clergy to comply with them, and the resolutions commanded the obedience, if not in every case the agreement, of the vast majority of the clergy.[40]

The Lambeth Conference resolutions of 1948 reaffirmed in substance those of 1930, but there were certain significant differences: *(i)* the term 'indissoluble' as applied to the marriage-bond was avoided; *(ii)* the recommendation that no divorced person with a former partner living should be married with the rites of the Church was subject to the exception, 'unless it has been established that there exists no marriage-bond recognised by the Church' - the influence of the 1946 American Canons is evident here; and *(iii)* no distinction was made

37 Winnett, op. cit. p. 225. 38. Ibid., p. 231.

39. Cf. the words of Archbishop Lang of Canterbury to the Upper House in January, 1937: 'These Resolutions of Convocation are not binding upon members of Convocation, or upon the Church generally, in the sense that to disregard them would be an act of disloyalty to the Church, but even in their present form they have a real authority as expressing the mind of Convocation. Those who accept and act upon these Resolutions know that they have this measure of authority behind them; those who decide not to accept and act upon them have the responsibility of setting this measure of authority aside. *Chronicle of Convocation,* 1935. p. 339.

40. The instruction of one bishop to his clergy read: 'My direction (in accordance with the resolutions passed by Convocation) is that no divorced person whose former partner is still alive shall be married with the Church's Marriage Service. Every clergyman has full legal liberty to refuse to solemnise such a marriage, and I direct him to refuse.'

between innocent and guilty divorced persons seeking admission to Communion.

The draft Canons of 1947 contained a provision (Canon XXXVIII., Section 1) that 'no person who has already been married but whose marriage has been dissolved by secular authority shall marry, except as provided by Canon XXXVI., so long as the husband or wife to whom that person was married is still living.'[41] This was altered by the Convocations to:

'No person who has already been married but whose marriage has been dissolved by secular authority shall be married according to the rites and ceremonies of the Church of England so long as the husband or wife to whom the person was married is still living.'

At the May 1956 session of the Canterbury Convocation the Archbishop pointed out the difficulties which the enactment of this part of the Canon would encounter when petition was made for the Royal Assent. It would entail a change in statute law, a section of the clergy would be aggrieved at being deprived of a liberty which the existing law allowed them and which for conscientious reasons they valued, and when the proposed Canon came under the scrutiny of Parliament, the sympathy of Parliament would be with the aggrieved clergy. It would be unwise, said the Archbishop, to seek a battle with Parliament on this particular issue, and such a battle 'would certainly not assist the cause but would set it back a very long way'. The proposed Canon was therefore withdrawn, but the Archbishop was at pains to emphasise that this did not lessen the spiritual authority of the Reso-

41. Canon XXXVI of the draft Canons contained a provision that the Bishop sitting with his Chancellor might, if satisfied that there were good grounds for regarding a dissolved marriage as in fact a case of nullity, allow either party to be remarried in church during the lifetime of the other. This part of the Canon was later withdrawn.

The views of the clergy may be gauged from the following: In September 1947 this question was put to the clergy of the Chelmsford Diocesan Synod: 'It is suggested that, in the case of the innocent party in a divorce for adultery, if such party is a regular communicant, after a period (e.g. two years) that person may be remarried in church. Do you agree with this proposal?' The voting was: Yes, 188; No, 189. Aprevious question asked in general terms concerning the remarriage in church of the innocent party. Here the vote was: Yes, 81; No, 357. *Chelmsford Diocesan Chronicle,* Nov. 1947. In the Diocese of London in 1947, 290 incumbents thought that the Church ought to refuse to solemnise the marriage of divorced persons in every case. 218 were against invariable refusal - but the question was put with special reference to the setting up of Church Courts to consider applications for remarriage. *Our Day of Opportunity* (Bishop of London's Charge, 1947).

lutions of Convocation, and on 1st October, 1957 the Archbishop declared Resolutions (1). to (4). of 1938 and the Resolutions on the Pastoral Care of the Divorced of 1956-57 to be an Act of Convocation.[42] The Act of Convocation, which brought together and unified the above-mentioned Resolutions, read as follows:

1 That this House reaffirms the following four Resolutions of 1938, and in place of Resolutions 5 then provisionally adopted by the Upper House substitutes Resolution 2 (A) below, which restates the procedure generally followed since 1938.

(1) That this House affirms that according to God's will, declared by our Lord, marriage is in its true principle a personal union, for better or for worse, of one man with one woman, exclusive of all others on either side, and indissoluble save by death.

(2) That this House also affirms as a consequence that remarriage after divorce during the lifetime of a former partner always involves a departure from the principles of marriage true as declared by our Lord.

(3) That in order to maintain the principle of lifelong obligation which is inherent in every legally contracted marriage and is expressed in the plainest terms in the Marriage Service, the Church should not allow the use of that Service in the case of anyone who has a partner still living.

(4) That while affirming its adherence to our Lord's principle and standard of marriage as stated in the first and second of the above resolutions, this House recognises that the actual discipline of particular Christian Communions in this matter has varied widely from time to time and place to place, and holds that the Church of England is competent to enact such a discipline of its own in regard to marriage as may from time to time appear most salutary and efficacious.

42. Winnett, op. cit. pp. 233 and 246-7. An Act of Convocation is thus described by Dr. Paul Welsby: 'When it is not desired to legislate by Canon, Convocation may make regulations by means of Acts of Convocation. Such an Act is a resolution passed by both Houses in identical terms and finally sanctioned and proclaimed by the Archbishop as President. It does not require the Royal Assent and it has no legal or constitutional force, but it is to be regarded as carrying considerable spiritual authority as embodying the mind, will and opinion of the Church as expressed through its authorised representatives in Convocation, and it is therefore entitled to the obedience and loyalty of the clergy of the province.' *How the Church of England Works,* p. 112.

2 (A) Recognising that the Church's pastoral care for all people includes those who during the lifetime of a former partner contract a second union, this House approves the following pastoral regulations as being the most salutary in present circumstances:

(a) When two persons have contracted a marriage in civil law during the lifetime of a former partner of either of them, and either or both desire to be baptized or confirmed or to partake of the Holy Communion, the incumbent or other priest having the cure of their souls shall refer the case to the Bishop of the diocese, with such information as he has and such recommendations as he may desire to make.

(b) The Bishop in considering the case shall give due weight to the preservation of the Church's witness to our Lord's standard of marriage and to the pastoral care of those who have departed from it.

(c) If the Bishop is satisfied that the parties concerned are in good faith and that their receiving of the Sacraments would be for the good of their souls and ought not to be a cause of offence to the Church, he shall signify his approval thereof both to the priest and to the party or parties concerned: this approval shall be given in writing and shall be accepted as authoritative both in the particular diocese and in all other dioceses of the province.

2 (B) No public Service shall be held for those who have contracted a civil marriage after divorce. It is not within the competence of the Convocations to lay down what private prayers the curate in the exercise of his pastoral Ministry may say with the persons concerned, or to issue regulations as to where or when these prayers shall be said.

2 (C) Recognising that pastoral care may well avert the danger of divorce if it comes into play before legal proceedings have been started, this House urges all clergy in their preparation of couples for marriage to tell them, both for their own sakes and for that of their friends, that the good offices of the clergy are always available.

The Lower House, in thanking the Archbishop for promulging the Resolutions as an Act of Convocation called upon the clergy to give the Act 'their loyal and unstinted allegiance in word and deed'.

The division of opinion in the Church of England concerning divorce and remarriage, which manifested itself in the years following the Reformation, continued right into the present century. Both indissolubilist and non-indissolubilist viewpoints found expression in the literature of the subject as well as in the debates of the Convocations.[43] But while agreement might be lacking in doctrine, virtual uniformity was reached in practice, thanks to the innate loyalty of the vast majority of the clergy and the recognition that was accorded to the Church's spiritual authority represented by the bishops and the Convocations. The Act of Convocation of 1957 embodied this working consensus.[44]

Appendix to Chapter I

LAMBETH CONFERENCE RESOLUTIONS ON DIVORCE AND REMARRIAGE

1888

4. (A). That, inasmuch as our Lord's words expressly forbid Divorce, except in the case of fornication or adultery, the Christian Church cannot recognise Divorce in any other than the accepted case, or give any sanction to the marriage of any person who has been divorced contrary to this law, during the life of the other party.

(B). That under no circumstances ought the guilty party, in the case of a divorce for fornication or adultery, to be regarded, during the lifetime of the innocent party, as a fit recipient of the Church on marriage.

(C). That, recognising the fact that there has always been a difference of opinion in the Church on the question whether our Lord meant to forbid marriage to the innocent party in a

43. On the indissolubilist side, K. E. Kirk, *Marriage and Divorce* (1st edition, 1933; second edition, 1948); R. C. Mortimer's revision of T. A. Lacey's *Marriage in Church and State,* (1947); R. Haw, *The State of Matrimony,* (1952). On the non-indissolubilist side, W. R. Inge, *Christian Ethics and Modern Problems,* (1930); J. H. Cruse and B. S. W. Green, *Marriage, Divorce and Repentance in the Church of England,* (1949); D. S. Bailey, *The Mystery of Love and Marriage,* (1952).

44. Practice in the Northern Province was governed by the Resolutions passed by the York Convocation in 1938. *Acts of the Convocations of Canterbury and York,* pp. 90-91.

divorce for adultery, the Conference recommends that the clergy should not be instructed to refuse the Sacraments or other privileges of the Church to those who, under civil sanction, are thus married.

1908

39. [Reaffirmation of the Resolution of 1888.]

40. When an innocent person has by means of a court of law divorced a spouse for adultery and desires to enter into another contract of marriage, it is undesirable that such a contract should receive the blessing of the Church. (Passed by 87 votes to 84.)

1920

67. The Conference affirms as our Lord's principle and standard of marriage a lifelong and indissoluble union, for better for worse, of one man with one woman, to the exclusion of all others on either side, and calls on all Christian people to maintain and bear witness to this standard.

Nevertheless the Conference admits the right of a national or regional Church within our Communion to deal with cases which fall within the exception mentioned in the record of our Lord's words in St. Matthew's Gospel, under provisions which such Church may lay down.

The Conference, while recognising the extreme difficulty of governments in framing marriage laws for citizens many of whom do not accept the Christian standard, expresses its firm belief that in every country the Church should be free to bear witness to that standard through its powers of administration and discipline exercised in relation to its own members.

1930

10. The Conference believes that in the exalted view of marriage taught by our Lord is to be found the solution of the problems with which we are faced. His teaching is reinforced by certain elements which have found a new emphasis in modern life, particularly the sacredness of personality, the more equal partnership of men and women, and the biological importance of monogamy.

11. The Conference believes that it is with this ideal in view that the Church must deal with questions of divorce and with whatever threatens the security of woman and the stability of the

home. Mindful of our Lord's words, 'What therefore God hath joined together, let not man put asunder', it reaffirms 'as our Lord's principle and standard of marriage . . . bear witness to this standard,' (As in 1920 Resolution).

In cases of divorce

(a). The Conference, while passing no judgment on the practice of regional or national Churches within our Communion, recommends that the marriage of one whose former partner is still living should not be celebrated according to the rites of the Church.

(b). Where an innocent person has remarried under civil sanction and desires to receive the Holy Communion, it recommends that the case should be referred for consideration to the Bishop, subject to provincial regulations.

(c). Finally, it would call attention to the Church's unceasing responsibility for the spiritual welfare of all her members who have come short of her standard in this as in any other respect, and to the fact that the Church's aim, individually and socially, is reconciliation to God and redemption from sin. It therefore urges all Bishops and clergy to keep this aim before them.

1948

92. Faced with the great increase in the number of broken marriages and the tragedy of children deprived of true home life, this Conference desires again to affirm that marriage always entails a lifelong union and obligation; it is convinced that upon the faithful observance of this divine law depend the stability of home life, the happiness of children and the real health of society. It calls upon members of the Church and others to do their utmost by word and example to uphold the sanctity of the marriage-bond and to counteract those influences which tend to destroy it. It is convinced that maintenance of the Church's standard of discipline can alone meet the deepest needs of men; and it earnestly implores those whose marriage, perhaps through no fault of their own, is unhappy to remain steadfastly faithful to their marriage vows.

94. The Conference affirms that the marriage of one whose former partner is still living may not be celebrated according to the rites of the Church, unless it has been established that there exists no marriage bond recognised by the Church.

95. Mindful of the needs of those who are in deep distress and claim the Church's sympathy, the Conference urges that provincial and regional Churches should consider how best their pastoral responsibility towards those who do not conform to our Lord's standard can be discharged.

96. Confirmed members of the Church who marry contrary to the law of the Church, as accepted in the provincial or regional Church to which they belong, should be regarded as subject to the discipline of the Church in respect of admission to Holy Communion. Their admission to Holy Communion lies within the discretion of the Bishop, due regard being had to their own spiritual good and the avoidance of scandal to others. It is important that the practice within each province or regional Church in this matter should be uniform. We restate Resolution 11 (b). of the Lambeth Conference, 1930, as follows: 'That in every case where a person with a former partner still living is remarried and desires to be admitted to Holy Communion the case should be referred to the Bishop, subject to provincial or regional regulations.'

97. Inasmuch as easy divorce in Great Britain, the United States and elsewhere, has gravely weakened the idea of the lifelong nature of marriage, and has also brought untold suffering to children, this Conference urges that there is a strong case for the reconsideration by certain States of their divorce laws.

1958

118. The Conference recognises that divorce is granted by the secular authority in many lands on grounds which the Church cannot acknowledge, and recognises also that in certain cases where a decree of divorce has been sought and may even have been granted, there may in fact have been no marital bond in the eyes of the Church. It therefore commends for further consideration by the Churches and Provinces of the Anglican Communion a procedure for defining marital status, such as already exists in some of its Provinces.

119. The Conference believes that the Resolutions of the 1948 Lambeth Conference concerning marriage discipline have been of great value as witnessing to Christ's teaching about the lifelong nature of marriage, and urges that these Resolutions, and their implications, should continue to be studied in every Province.

II.

DIVORCE AND REMARRIAGE IN RECENT ANGLICAN THOUGHT

In 1955 the Archbishop of Canterbury, Dr. Geoffrey Fisher, now Archbishop Lord Fisher of Lambeth, delivered an address to a group of City men, which was later published under the title, *Problems of Marriage and Divorce.* This pamphlet remains the clearest and most authoritative exposition of the marriage discipline of the Church of England as expressed in the resolutions of the Lambeth Conferences and the Convocations. The refusal of marriage with the Church's rites to divorced persons with a partner still living, coupled with their admission to Communion at the discretion of the bishop, has frequently been regarded as an illogical compromise, but the Archbishop holds that it represents a genuine attempt to translate into practice what our Lord taught about marriage. Our Lord, in declaring marriage to be a lifelong union, was not setting forth an 'ideal' but stating what marriage essentially is in the divine intention.[1] For this reason the Church cannot solemnise the marriage of divorced persons with a partner still living without ceasing to bear witness to what Christ affirmed marriage to be. Such remarriage, while not 'adultery' in the commonly accepted sense of the word, is nevertheless 'adultery' when judged in the light of the divine will.[2]

But if our Lord was not setting forth an ideal, neither was he legislating in the sense of laying down rules or a code of discipline for his Church. Rather he left the Church to frame its own discipline under the guidance of the Holy Spirit, having regard to the conditions under which marriage exists in a sinful world. The Pauline Privilege,[3] and probably also the Exceptive Clause in St. Matthew, are instances of the way in which from the beginning the Church felt free to deal with practical problems as they arose.[4] Every part of Christendom has developed its own form of marriage discipline, and in the opinion of the Archbishop that of the Church of England is 'the nearest to

1. *Problems of Marriage and Divorce,* p. 8.
2. Ibid. p. 12.
3. St. Paul's ruling in I Corinthians 7. 15 (which he distinguishes from a word of the Lord) that a Christian convert deserted by a heathen spouse is 'not under bondage', which has generally been interpreted as implying a freedom to marry again, 'in the Lord'.
4. *Problems of Marriage and Divorce,* pp. 10-11.

Christ's will because it deals as little as possible in legalities and courts and as largely as possible in terms of moral and spiritual truth'.[5] In admitting divorced and remarried persons to the sacraments the Church is following the example of Christ in seeking and saving the lost and in bringing them into a living relationship with himself. To tell them that as a condition of admission they must disregard accepted obligations, break up a home, and commit themselves to lifelong celibacy, would mean a failure to help them and a frustration of the Holy Spirit's work in their lives.[6] The Archbishop frankly acknowledges that 'in some cases where a first marriage has ended in tragedy, a second marriage has, by every test of the Holy Spirit that we are able to recognise, been abundantly blessed'.[7]

Archbishop Lord Fisher must be reckoned among those who take the indissolubilist view of marriage, although he does not use the word 'indissoluble' but rather 'lifelong', and he recognises that a second marriage after divorce, while in its origin representing a falling short of God's will, may nevertheless by the blessing of God and the grace of the Holy Spirit, become a true marriage.

A small book, entitled *Marriage*, by Walter Boulton, at that time Provost of Guildford, appeared in 1960. Here again the principle of indissoluble marriage was clearly stated, at least in respect of the marriages of Christians. When two Christians enter into marriage, in full understanding of what the Christian view of marriage is, 'then it is a true marriage, it is lifelong, and divorce is not merely undesirable, it is impossible. Whatever the State may claim to do, it cannot dissolve the marriage, and any so-called remarriage, however hard we try to dress it up in legal respectability, in Christian eyes is plain adultery.'[8] But in view of the fact that many do not accept the Christian view of marriage, and of the facilities which the State provides for the termination of marriage, not all marriages can be presumed to be lifelong in intention, and where there is good reason to suppose that one or both of the parties entered into it with a lack of true Christian intention, the marriage, if ended by divorce, should be treated as void and therefore not a barrier to a second, and Christian, marriage with the Church's blessing. Mr. Boulton advocated the setting up of Church

5. Ibid., p. 20.
6. Ibid., p. 30.
7. Ibid., p. 23.
8. *Marriage* (revised edition), p. 65.

Courts to consider such cases, on the lines suggested earlier by Dr. Mortimer.[9]

An important contribution to the theology of marriage was made by Gordon Dunstan, of the Church of England Moral Welfare Council,[10] in a sermon before the University of Cambridge in November, 1960, entitled *The Marriage Covenant.* Against a 'low' doctrine of marriage, which bases marriage on a contract between the parties, and a 'high' doctrine which finds the essence of marriage in the 'one-flesh' union identified with sexual intercourse, the preacher maintained that a Biblical and Christian doctrine of marriage must interpret marriage in terms of a covenant. The covenant of marriage must be seen in the light of the covenant of God with Israel and of Christ with his Church.[11] In the covenant of marriage, as in the covenants of the Bible, there are present these elements: the initiative of love which creates a relationship between lover and beloved; a moral affirmation or oath; the commandments of fidelity and mutual care; the blessings promised to faithfulness and obedience; and sacrifice, or death to the old life and the rising again to a new.[12] To distinguish between an 'institutional' marriage effected by exchange of vows, and an 'ontological' marriage established by intercourse 'strikes out', in Professor Dunstan's words, 'a whole dimension of man by denying the effectiveness of the moral element in his personality. An "essential change in the character of personal relation" can be and is effected by a vow, by the sort of moral affirmation which creates covenanted relationships . . . We do no honour to the physical bond in marriage by enfeebling the moral bond, the unitive power of the pledged word.'[13] The thesis of Professor Dunstan's sermon was developed by Professor V. A. Demant in his small book, *An Exposition*

9. Ibid., pp. 71-72. Lacey-Mortimer, *Marriage in Church and State,* p. 207. Mr. Boulton's book was originally published by the Mothers' Union, and the author was careful to state in his preface that his recommendation regarding Church Courts to consider cases of dissolved marriages was his own, and in no way committed the Mothers' Union. Shortly after publication, and following some controversy in the church press, the Mothers' Union withdrew the book from circulation, but a revised edition was published by S.P.C.K. in 1963. The revised edition, however, embodied no changes of substance and still contained the author's suggestions regarding Church Courts.

10. Now Maurice Professor of Moral and Social Theology at King's College, London.

11. *The Marriage Covenant,* pp. 3-6.

12. Ibid., pp. 7-12.

13. Ibid., p. 14. For the 'coital' view of marriage which is here under criticism see D. Sherwin Bailey, *The Mystery of Love and Marriage,* esp. pp. 45-47.

of Christian Sex Ethics (1963). The interpretation of marriage in terms of a covenant and in the light of the covenants of God with man necessarily implies that permanence, in the sense of lifelong love and fidelity, is of the essence of marriage, but neither Professor Dunstan nor Professor Demant goes on to discuss the practical question of what the Church should do when a marriage has broken down and ended in divorce, and a new union is contemplated or has taken place.

Divorce and remarriage is the subject of a chapter in Helen Oppenheimer's book, *Law and Love,* an original and penetrating study of the ethical teaching of Christ, and the subtlety of her thought is such that she cannot be classed as an upholder *tout simple* of either the indissolubilist or the non-indissolubilist position. As against the rigorists who contend that Christ laid down a code of rules, and the 'liberals' who see in his teaching only general principles and ideals to show us the spirit in which we ought to act, Lady Oppenheimer maintains that Christ did give us definite precepts, but precepts which are to be interpreted in the context not of a morality of rights and duties, but of a family life in which love goes beyond, and transcends, considerations of rights and duties. Christian morality is the way of life of the family of God: 'it is the way people live when they are conscious of being the children of God'.[14]

The question of divorce and remarriage affords an illustration of the distinctive character of Christ's ethical teaching. In her chapter, 'An Illustration: the Problem of Divorce', Lady Oppenheimer discusses with great insight three views on divorce and remarriage held in the Church of England and their points of strength and weakness. The 'two standards' view, which distinguishes between Christian marriages and marriages which have only civil sanction, may appear to fit in with the facts of contemporary society, but it ignores a fundamental element in Christian teaching about marriage, namely, that as Christ went back behind the Mosaic permission of divorce to God's intention in the original creation, so indissolubility is not a peculiar or superadded characteristic of Christian marriages, but pertains in the will of God to all marriages. The 'pastoral' view accepts indissolubility as an ideal, yet allows that in certain circumstances a second marriage after divorce may be the will of God for the individuals concerned. This view, says Lady Oppenheimer, 'avoids rigorism but not legalism', for the Church clearly cannot give its blessing to all second

14. *Law and Love,* p. 33.

marriages after divorce, and means of discrimination between one case and another must be found; and it is open to the further objection that it hardly squares with the undoubted and uncompromising teaching of Christ. The third or 'rigorist' view is equally open to objection. It seeks to hold fast to the teaching of Christ, but it makes an impossible demand when it faces those who have remarried after divorce with the alternative of breaking the promises and abandoning the responsibilities of the second marriage, of 'living as brother and sister', or being permanently cut off from the Church. The rigorist view, moreover, is bound up with a legalism which can make a decision in hard cases depend not on the moral situation but on luck, as when the fact of baptism or non-baptism in infancy determines whether or not the Pauline Privilege can be pleaded to permit a new marriage in Church.[15]

At this point Lady Oppenheimer recalls us to a consideration of what Christ's ethical teaching is. 'Just as human love asks more of us than can "reasonably" be expected, so does the teaching of Christ. It cannot therefore be enforced as law, or injustice will be the only result. It can only be kept if law is transcended and the spirit of love is achieved, and to this there is no legal or even dutiful short-cut.' Christ's teaching on divorce is of the same kind as his teaching on anger, retaliation, lust and going to law. The question of remarriage after divorce is on the same footing as that of the Christian's right to kill in self-defence or to claim damages for injury in a court of law. He may do it, his action will not be immoral, but he cannot say that he is doing it as a Christian. So, says Lady Oppenheimer,

> 'the man who has put away his wife and married again has insisted on his legal rights. This was a betrayal of the Christian spirit, and from the point of view of Christ's teaching he has committed adultery, but this does not mean that he is necessarily still in a quasi-legal state of "living in sin", any more than a man who has once brought a lawsuit against his enemies instead of forgiving them is considered to have stolen his own property because he did not make a present of it to his antagonists. The question of whether a man is living sinfully depends upon the spirit in which he is living now, not upon the spirit in which he has acted in the past, still less upon the events beyond his control, such as whether or not he was baptised as a baby.'[16]

15. Ibid., pp. 67-72. 16. Ibid., p. 76.

On the practical issue of church discipline Lady Oppenheimer considers that the Church is right in not allowing second marriages after divorce to take place with the Church's rites, for the Church 'can hardly give its formal blessing to people when they are actually doing what Christ particularly wished them not to do'. At the same time, however, the Church should fully recognise a civil marriage in these cases as a valid marriage, and 'it should not regard a failure to uphold the Christian spirit in marriage as necessarily a ground for excommunication any more than a failure to uphold the Christian spirit in trade'.[17] A sacrament is a means of grace, not a prize for good conduct; and to refuse it as a penal measure is wrong and unchristian.

Lady Oppenheimer clearly holds that only the concept of marriage as indissoluble meets the demands of Christ's teaching, yet this teaching is not to be regarded as a law, but rather as a call to transcend law. By her fresh approach to the question of divorce and remarriage she has lifted the discussion into a larger dimension than that in which it has generally hitherto taken place.

Another example of an adherence to the principle of indissolubility which nevertheless avoids the extreme of rigorism is afforded by Canon H. M. Waddams in his book, *A New Introduction to Moral Theology* (1964). He defends the decisions of the Convocations as wise practically though difficult to defend logically. They aim at 'making a public witness against second marriages, though continuing to minister to the souls which need pastoral care.'[18] 'Remarriage after divorce is always wrong for Christians', writes Canon Waddams, but he adds, 'There are cases where the alternative is morally worse.' A typical example is that of a husband after divorce with the custody of young children: it may be his duty to remarry in order that his children may have maternal care. However, the fact that the second marriage may be morally the right course does not mean that it should be solemnised in church, but rather 'those concerned should accept as their contribution to the maintenance of lifelong marriage as an ideal and standard the need to forego a church wedding'.[19]

Turning now to those who unequivocally reject the indissolubilist position, we would first call attention to Canon A. P. Shepherd's small but closely reasoned book, *Marriage was Made for Man* (1958). The book opens with an attack on the Act of Convocation of 1957, and the resolutions it embodies, as an attempt to deprive the clergy of a liberty which rightfully belongs to them, and to impose an ex-

17. Ibid., p. 78. 18. Op. cit., p. 136. 19. Ibid., p. 137.

communication upon a whole class of innocent people, to be lifted only by episcopal permit. Canon Shepherd would go even further and declare the Act of Convocation illegal as contravening the Submission of the Clergy Act of Henry VIII, which forbade the Convocations to enact any canons or constitutions, 'by whatsoever name or names they may be called', without the royal licence and assent.[20]

Canon Shepherd next proceeds to consider the teaching of Christ on marriage. He maintains that the words of Christ in Mark 10. 9 should be translated 'What God hath joined together, let not a husband put asunder'; what is here disallowed is the right of a man to end his own marriage, not the dissolution of a marriage on adequate grounds by a competent authority.[21] What Christ has in mind is the laxity of certain rabbis who held that a man might divorce his wife if he found another woman more attractive. So the saying, 'Whosoever shall put away his wife and marry another, commits adultery' must be understood to mean, 'Whosoever shall put away his wife in order to marry another commits adultery, even though he seeks to regularise it by a bill of divorce.' But this is not to say that for Christ marriage was indissoluble, for the Exceptive Clause in Matthew (which Canon Shepherd accepts as an authentic word of Christ) makes it clear that in one case at least, namely unfaithfulness, divorce is lawful, and St. Paul's direction concerning a Christian convert deserted by a non-Christian spouse shows that he did not understand the teaching of Christ as totally forbidding divorce.[22]

On the positive side Canon Shepherd approves the attitude of the Eastern Orthodox Churches to divorce, pointing out that it represents less a concession to the state than a genuine attempt to express the Christian standard of marriage in legislation which takes account of human frailty and imperfection. The Orthodox view combines a high conception of the personal and spiritual aspects of marriage with compassion for those who have failed to achieve the ideal, and there is granted them after divorce the opportunity of another attempt to enter into a true and lasting marriage. In Canon Shepherd's words, the Orthodox attitude is a 'mixture of extreme idealism with compassionate realism'.[23]

20. *Marriage was made for Man,* p. 37.
21. Ibid., pp. 44-45. But while *anthropos* in certain contexts can mean a married man or husband, the fact that in this verse it is set over against God would suggest that human agency in general is meant.
22. Ibid., pp. 53-55;
23. Ibid., p. 111.

Rejecting the present discipline of the Church of England Canon Shepherd sees as a preferable alternative the Church's mediation in cases where there is a threat of marriage breakdown. 'What is needed', he says, 'is that churchpeople should recognise that if they are married in church and with Christian rites, they have involved the Church in the sanctity of their vows, and if the marriage breaks down the Church is involved in their tragedy. It is their duty to seek the help of the Church at the first threat of such a breakdown.' Marriages in church should be solemnised subject to an undertaking that the parties should seek the aid and counsel of the Church, as represented by the parish priest or bishop, whenever circumstances arise to endanger the stability of the marriage. Those who had sought this help from the Church would, in the event of failure and a divorce taking place, be eligible for remarriage with the blessing of the Church. Those who had neglected to seek this help should not, unless there were special reasons and penitence were shown, be deemed eligible.[24]

According to Dr. Sherwin Bailey in *Common Sense about Sexual Ethics: a Christian View* (1962), the doctrine of the indissolubility of marriage, as distinct from the doctrine that marriage is in principle permanent, is 'essentially speculative'. It can claim no support from the teaching of Jesus, though Jesus clearly regarded divorce and remarriage as involving a breach of God's purpose for marriage and as such meriting the condemnation due to adultery.[25] But to convert an ethical principle into a legislative prohibition is contrary to the whole spirit of the Gospel, and 'the fact must be faced that relational breakdown in marriage is sometimes absolute and impossible to repair'. The idea of a *vinculum* or bond apart from the common life of husband and wife is for Dr. Bailey (as it was for Bishop Hall and Bishop Cosin) no more than a metaphysical abstraction or figment, and he asks what good is served by pretending, when the personal relationship in marriage has broken down, that a marriage is still essentially in being. Certainly a separation which excludes remarriage may allow for the possibility of forgiveness and the taking back of an erring partner, but this does not apply to 'a case of deep relational disintegration which even repentance and forgiveness cannot heal'.[26]

24. Ibid., pp. 82-86. The 1957 Act of Convocation in Regulation 2 (C) places upon the clergy the responsibility for telling couples who they prepare for marriage that 'the good offices of the clergy are always available' in cases of marriage difficulties.
25. *Common Sense about Sexual Ethics: a Christian View,* p. 170.
26. Ibid., p. 172.

Dr. Bailey's conclusion is that in cases where a marriage has irretrievably broken down both Church and State must deal with the problem 'constructively and compassionately, with the object of bringing out of the evil situation whatever good is possible, and in many cases a successful second marriage will be the most creative form of reparation for past failure.'[27]

What has come to be known as the 'New Theology' has its counterpart in the so-called 'New Morality', and 'The New Morality' is the title of a chapter in the book by Dr. John Robinson, Bishop of Woolwich, *Honest to God,* whose publication in 1963 sparked off the liveliest theological controversy of modern times. In the Bishop's view the notion of the indissolubility of marriage, in the sense that marriage *cannot* be dissolved, is the relic of an outdated and untenable supernaturalism, according to which 'the network of empirical relationships is but a veil for a world of occult realities which lie behind the outward order of things and constitute the truth about man or society or nature, however much the empirical facts may appear to dispute it'.[28] On the supernaturalist view a marriage as a metaphysical reality exists independently of the personal relationship between the parties, and divorce is not merely wrong but impossible. Another version of the supernaturalist ethic, and one commonly held among Protestants, is that divorce is wrong because it is contrary to the absolute command of God, and if any concessions are made, it can only be because of the 'hardness of men's hearts'. Both these forms of supernaturalism must be rejected, says the Bishop, in favour of an 'ethic of the situation', in which nothing is prescribed except love and for which nothing is evil except lack of love. Divorce is not wrong in itself, but only in so far as it is contrary to the demands of love and to the deepest welfare of the particular persons in their particular situation. So, in the words of Professor Joseph Fletcher quoted by the Bishop, 'If the emotional and spiritual welfare of both parents and children in a particular family can be served best by a divorce, wrong and cheapjack as divorce commonly is, then love requires it.'[29]

27. Ibid., p. 175.

28. *Honest to God,* p. 107, Dr. Robinson refers to Mr. John Wren-Lewis's article, 'The Decline of Magic in Art and Politics' (*Critical Quarterly,* Spring 1960), though Mr. Wren-Lewis does not cite the changed conception of marriage as an illustration of his thesis.

29. Ibid., p. 118. The quotation is from an article, 'The New Look in Christian Ethics', *Harvard Divinity Bulletin,* October 1959. Professor Fletcher, an American Episcopalian, writes in his book, *Situation Ethics,* p. 133: 'Love's method is to judge by particularity, not to lay down laws and universals. It does not preach pretty propositions; it asks concrete questions, situation questions.

The question of divorce is further discussed by the Bishop of Woolwich in his Liverpool Cathedral lectures published under the title of *Christian Morals Today* (1964). The Bishop finds the essence of Jesus' ethic in 'unconditional neighbour-love', which can never be translated into law, but only illustrated by parables or dramatic pictures such as we have in the Sermon on the Mount. 'Turning the other cheek' cannot be made a law, and the same is true of the sayings concerning marriage. If divorce according to Jesus is the moral equivalent of adultery, so equally is lustful desire, and no one has thought of treating the saying of Jesus about lust as legislation.[30] Again whether divorce in every case is right or wrong is held to depend upon what love demands in the situation: 'the factors to be taken into account - the wreck of the personal relationship, the children, the third parties involved, the vows, the weakening of the marriage nexus in society, etc. - all these are part of the agonising calculation to be made. But ultimately, when love's account has been done, it must be *this* that is decisive, not something prescribed from without in advance.'[31]

From the same diocese as that in which the Bishop of Woolwich serves came a book by Canon Douglas Rhymes, *No New Morality* (1964), based on a series of sermons preached in Southwark Cathedral. Canon Rhymes finds the present position of the Church of England in respect of divorce and remarriage unsatisfactory for three reasons. First, it implies that a second marriage after divorce cannot be a true marriage, even when it is clear that the first marriage was a mistake and the second marriage shows all the marks of a true Christian marriage. Secondly, it means, in Canon Rhymes's words, that 'we are placed in the strangely ironic position of being better able to deal with those who break our laws and then come to us than with those who ask our advice in advance'. We can deal compassionately with the former and allow them to enter into the life of the Church, but to the latter we can only present the alternatives of continuing in a union from which all reality has departed or resigning themselves to lifelong continence. Thirdly, by our approval of separation but condemnation of divorce we overlook the fact that separation itself 'destroys the whole spirit of the indissolubility of marriage'.[32]

The Church, says Canon Rhymes, must face the fact of marriage

32. *No New Morality*, pp. 65-66. 30. Ibid., pp. 24-25. 31. Ibid., p. 43.

Getting a divorce is sometimes like David's eating the reserved Sacrament: it is what Christ would recommend.'

breakdown realistically and cease insisting that 'what is dead must be made to look alive'. The Church should publicly recognise that a marriage can become a hollow shell with all personal relationship gone out of it, and in cases where the Church has solemnised the marriage, the Church should formally absolve the partners from their vows, just as absolution can be granted from monastic vows. Consideration might also be given to an extension of nullity, for if a marriage has completely broken down it could mean that essential elements of the marriage-union were never present and that it was never really a Christian marriage. Finally, the Church should cease to insist, as it has done in the past, that its own minority view of marriage should be reflected in the law of the state.[33]

Dr. F. R. Barry, formerly Bishop of Southwell, has given us the first-fruits of his retirement in his book, *Christian Ethics and Secular Society* (1966), in which the problem of divorce and remarriage is discussed with the wisdom and insight characteristic of the author. 'Marriage', he says, 'presupposes a lifelong union, and indeed the irrevocability of the vows is one of its strongest defences and supports. A marriage that starts with the back-door left open will be in danger at every difficult turning, when instead of helping one another round it, the couple decide "it doesn't work" and separate.' Yet if in intention marriage is a lifelong union, marriages do in fact break down, and in that case, asks Dr. Barry, 'is the cause of marriage best served by holding together in a legal tie two people whose love has turned to hate, where the moral realities of marriage have altogether ceased to exist?'[34] The Church has always recognised separation, but the question is whether remarriage should be allowed, and on this Dr. Barry says:

> 'Once the original marriage has broken down there is set in motion a train of consequences in which no ideally right course is any longer within the reach of either party. What is morally right for them now is to do the best that *can* be done in the circumstances. To tell them that they must now live as celibates is either to invite fornication or to put a strain on human nature that can only be endured by heroic sanctity. These poor people have often been terribly wounded by the failure of the first, hopeful marriage and the subsequent ignominy of the divorce court. They often hate themselves and are deeply penitent (even the guilty party) for their

33. Ibid., pp. 75-77.
34. *Christian Ethics and Secular Society*, pp. 204-6.

share in it. If a new marriage now comes within their reach in which they can find true love and a fresh start, some new faith and growth in Christian character - and the second marriage often does bring these things - may not this be the way of healing and forgiveness?'[35]

Dr. Barry would make ecclesiastical discipline take second place to the pastoral care which would help to make the second marriage a truly Christian marriage.

The most recent contribution to the debate on the non-indissolubilist side is the pamphlet comprising two lectures by Canon Hugh Montefiore, of Cambridge, and entitled *Remarriage and Mixed Marriage: a Plea for Dual Reform.* (1967). Canon Montefiore is uncompromising, and some would say unfair, in his criticism of the present marriage discipline of the Church of England, which, he says, 'is typical of the mushy and woolly thinking to be found in the Church of England, especially in its higher reaches. We try to eat our cake and have it, and we justify it by the blessed phrase "pastoral expediency".'[36] The author brings the doctrine of indissolubility to the test of the three Anglican criteria of Scripture, Reason and Tradition. Scripture affords no support for the doctrine, for Jesus did not legislate on marriage, and the Matthaean Exception shows that when Jesus' ethical demands are turned into legislation there is a case for divorce and remarriage in certain circumstances.[37] On grounds of reason marriage cannot be held to be indissoluble since in fact marriages are dissolved, and in these cases remarriage should be permissible when it 'serves better to godliness' and it 'would produce worse results in Christian disobedience not to remarry'.[38] Not all are able to live in continence, and sexual frustration can manifest itself in selfishness, greed and other deadly sins. Nor, says Canon Montefiore, can tradition be appealed to in support of indissolubility, for the Christian Church has at many periods and in many places permitted divorce with remarriage, of which the long-standing practice of the Eastern Churches is an example. Canon Montefiore views with approval the approach adopted by the Protestant Episcopal Church in the United States, and by the Anglican Church in Canada in its latest Marriage Canon, and he concludes: 'I suggest then that in suitable cases remarriage be permitted in England's parish churches, using the

35. Ibid., p. 208.
36. *Remarriage and Mixed Marriage,* p. 4.
37. Ibid., p. 10. 38. Ibid., p. 13.

same service as we have now, with a prayer added admitting failure in the past, praying for forgiveness, and asking for future blessing.'[39]

It will appear from the survey of opinion in this chapter that there is a movement in the Church of England away from the doctrine of the absolute indissolubility of marriage. Those who still uphold the general principle of indissolubility do so in a form which mitigates its strictness and in a manner which avoids a harsh rigorism and an unrealistic legalism. Many who regard themselves as still committed to the indissolubilist view, and therefore deem marriage after divorce to be wrong, would at the same time allow that in certain circumstances such remarriage could be the less wrong of two possible courses, and that many marriages after divorce bear all the marks of being blessed by God. A growing body of opinion would, however, question, and even reject, the doctrine of indissolubility and as a consequence call for a radical change in the present marriage discipline of the Church of England.

39. Ibid., p. 17.

III.

DIVORCE AND REMARRIAGE: THE ANGLICAN COMMUNION OUTSIDE ENGLAND

In this chapter the discipline concerning divorce and remarriage in the provinces of the Anglican Communion, other than those of the Church of England, will be considered, and changes occurring in recent years will be specially noted.

Practice in the Church in Wales is governed by the Letter of Advice to the Clergy from the Welsh bishops, first issued in 1938 and reissued in 1966. This directs that no marriage of a divorced person with a partner still living shall be solemnised in church, and that no divorced and remarried person shall receive Communion until permitted by the Bishop of the Diocese to do so. In a recent revision of the Marriage Service of the Church in Wales this statement was included: 'Marriage is a lifelong union of one man and one woman, and is dissolved only by the death of either party', and a Form for the Blessing of a Civil Marriage was prefaced by a rubric forbidding its use in the case of divorced persons remarrying during the lifetime of their former partners.

The Prayer Book of the Episcopal Church in Scotland prefaces its Marriage Service with a quotation from Canon XXX forbidding its use when one of the parties is divorced and remarries while his former partner is still alive. In the case of a divorced and remarried person seeking admission to Holy Communion the Rector of the parish lays the particulars before the Bishop of the Diocese, who consults the College of Bishops at their next meeting, and in the light of their advice admits, or refuses to admit, the applicant to Communion.

The matter of remarriage after divorce has never been before the General Synod of the Church of Ireland, but the Irish bishops will not allow the issue of marriage licences when one of the parties is divorced and has a spouse still living. A Pastoral Letter of the Bishops issued in November 1966, says of the Prayer Book Marriage Service that 'its language is uncompromising in that it emphasises the unity and indissolubility of the partnership. In a union consecrated by God the bride and bridegroom by free consent take each other as lifelong partners, "for better, for worse, till death us do part".' The Letter continues: 'The teaching of the Church of Ireland is that a divorced spouse is not permitted to be a partner in this Prayer Book Marriage Service during the lifetime of the other spouse.'[1]

The special circumstances existing in Middle Eastern countries, in many of which ecclesiastical courts exercise jurisdiction in divorce, and where many Christians are converts from non-Christian religions, are reflected in the following extract from the Regulations issued by the Archbishop and Bishops of the Jerusalem Archbishopric:

'B. 13. The Bishop cannot sanction the remarriage during the lifetime of their former partners of persons who have obtained a divorce or separation either from the civil courts or from the ecclesiastical courts of any other religious community. This ruling applies whether the original marriage was religious or civil, but the Bishop reserves to his individual decision cases that may arise of converts from Islam or Judaism who were married and divorced before their conversion.

14. No other Church has the right to issue a decree of divorce between two persons married in an Anglican Church.

15. Any question of admission to Holy Communion of persons divorced and remarried, of persons against whom a divorce has been granted by the civil courts or of persons married within degrees prohibited by the Church, should be referred to the Bishop'.

The practice of the Church of India, Pakistan, Burma and Ceylon is laid down in its *Constitution, Canons and Rules,* which were drawn up in 1930, confirmed in1953 and revised in 1960. Canon 4 of Chapter 26, 'Of Marriage', declares that those who marry contrary to the law of the Church are subject to the discipline of the Church in the matter of eligibility for Confirmation and admission to Holy Com-

1. The present Constitution of the Republic of Ireland contains a provision that 'no law shall be enacted providing for the grant of a dissolution of marriage'. Thus there is no divorce in the Republic. The Committee on the Constitution, which reported in December 1967, recommended that the provision in question should be replaced by one on the following lines: 'In the case of a person who was married in accordance with the rites of a religion, no law shall be enacted providing for the grant of a dissolution of that marriage on grounds other than those acceptable to that religion.' If this provision were adopted a marriage solemnised in a Roman Catholic church (or a Church of Ireland place of worship?) could not be dissolved, but one solemnised in a Presbyterian church could presumably be dissolved for adultery or desertion. It could also enable the State in Ireland to recognise the Roman Catholic dissolutions or annulments which at present it does not recognise.

munion. Canon 6, dealing with the marriage of divorced persons, reads as follows:

> 'A person who has already been married as a Christian and whose marriage has been dissolved by secular authority, or who having been married as a non-Christian has been received into the Church and whose marriage, then recognised, has been subsequently dissolved by secular authority, except as provided in Canon 7, may not marry so long as the husband or wife to whom that person was married is still living; and no minister of the Church shall perform such a marriage.'

Canon 7 provides that in cases where a marriage has been declared null by a civil court on grounds which are recognised by the Church the Bishop may certify that no marriage-bond as recognised by the Church exists, and that either party to the annulled marriage is free to contract a Christian marriage with another person.

Canon 26 declares the Pauline Privilege (I Corinthians 7. 15) to be operative in the case of a convert to Christianity deserted by a non-Christian spouse on account of his or her change of religion,

> 'provided that the marriage has been dissolved under any civil law regulating the dissolution of marriage of converts in any cases where it is applied or in accordance with any recognised law or custom, and the authorities of the Church are satisfied after direct interrogation that the non-Christian partner is unwilling either to be baptised or to continue in wedlock without interfering with the religious obligations of the convert'.

Rule 32 requires that those contemplating divorce proceedings first submit their case to the judgment of the Church in the hope of a reconciliation being effected. Rule 33 lays down that a divorced person, whether the innocent or the guilty party, who remarries during the former spouse's lifetime, forfeits the right of admission to Holy Communion. The clergy are required to report to the Bishop all cases of the remarriage of divorced persons, and no application for readmission to Holy Communion shall be considered by the Bishop until at least a year has elapsed after the remarriage. The purpose of suspension from Communion is 'both to testify to the fact that such marriages are contrary to the ideal set before Christian people and also to afford an opportunity of testing whether the applicants are genuinely determined to live together in a Christian way'. The Bishop may, however, exercise exceptional leniency if he is satisfied that an applicant was in no way to blame for the breakdown of the previous marriage.

In the Church of the Province of South Africa remarriage in church after divorce is forbidden by Canon XXIX, but most of the bishops of the Province have allowed remarried divorced persons to receive Communion after a period of discipline and after consideration of the case. In 1955 the Provincial Synod passed a Canon on Nullity, which provided that in each diocese a Nullity Court should be set up consisting of the Bishop and two persons appointed by the Chapter or Bishop's Senate, one a priest and the other a communicant layman learned in the law. The Nullity Court will consider applications only in cases where a marriage has been previously dissolved or annulled by a civil court, and the rules under which it is to act are laid down as follows: (A). Prohibited degrees, an existing marriage-bond recognised as such by the Church, and error as to identity render a marriage *ipso facto* void; (B). a marriage may be declared void by the Court on the following grounds: absence of proper formalities, lack of age according to civil law, absence of free consent through duress, mental deficiency, ignorance that a marriage was being performed, impotence, pregnancy by another man, and 'the fact that either of the parties (not being a catechumen) was unbaptised at the time of the marriage and that the unbaptised party is unwilling to regard the marriage as binding in the Christian sense'. Evidence given to the Court must be on oath, and the Court has power to withhold a decree 'if it be of opinion that the granting of it, though in accordance with ecclesiastical law, would be contrary to the principles of equity'.

In November, 1962, the Episcopal Synod of the Province of South Africa passed a resolution to the effect:

'(1). That it was undesirable to try to fix any general period of time after a second union had been contracted before the restoration of the parties involved to Communion could be contemplated.

(2). That dispensations given in such cases could only be strictly valid in the Diocese of the Bishop by whom they were issued; but that it might be undesirable to insist upon formal application by the persons concerned for a new dispensation whenever they moved to a new Diocese, on the ground that the Bishops respected one another's decisions in such matters.

(3). That those readmitted to Communion be also regarded as eligible for Church office'.

The Church of the Province of Central Africa in its Canons of 1962 prohibits by Canon XXII (3) a priest from solemnising the marriage of a divorced person during the former partner's lifetime, except in cases where a marriage has been declared null by a Diocesan Court. Canon XXIII, 'Of Nullity of Marriage', almost verbally reproduces the South African Canon on Nullity.

The Constitution of the Church of the Province of West Africa, which came into force in 1963, contains a Chapter on Marriage, whose opening statement declares marriage to be by divine institution 'a life-long and exclusive union and partnership between one man and one woman'. Canon I. (c) lays down that the Church's Form of Solemnisation of Holy Matrimony shall not be used 'in the case of a proposed marriage in which either of the parties shall have been married by Christian rites or by another form of monogamous marriage to a person or persons still living'. Nevertheless a person whose marriage has been civilly dissolved or annulled and who desires to remarry with the Church's rites during the former partner's lifetime may apply to the Bishop for a judgment (Canon I. (d). i), in which case judgment shall be given by the Bishop 'with the concurrence of the majority of two or more assessors sitting together or by correspondence with one or more of them'. (Canon I. (d). ii). The assessors are to include the Archdeacon of the Archdeaconry in which one or other of the parties resides and the Chancellor or Registrar of the Diocese, or some other communicant member learned in the law. No case shall be considered until at least a year after the civil decree has become final (Canon I. (d). iv). Subsection vii reads:

> 'Before a favourable judgment is rendered the Bishop and a majority of the assessors shall be satisfied:
>
> (a) That both parties are baptised;
>
> (b) that no facts exist which would make the proposed marriage bigamous;
>
> (c) that both parties do intend a Christian marriage;
>
> and *either:*
>
> (d) that one or more of the facts set forth in Schedule A of this Chapter are shown to have existed in the previous relationship of him/her whose marriage has been annulled or dissolved which manifestly establish that no marriage-bond as is recognised by the Church exists;
>
> *or*
>
> (e) that such defects of personality shall have been shown to

exist as to have made the continuance of the marriage impossible'.

The provision in (e) requires comment as it is not clear whether the judgment is one of nullity or divorce. The fact that the former marriage need not be a barrier to a second marriage in church suggests in the light of Canon I. (c) that the former marriage is held to be null. On the other hand the words 'continuance of the marriage' presuppose the existence of a marriage, and the fact that the defects of personality must be shown to 'exist' and not necessarily to have existed at the time of the marriage, would indicate that we have what is more properly a case of divorce. It would, of course, be possible to presume from the fact that defects of personality 'exist' that they were present in a latent form at the time of the marriage. The influence of Canon 18 of the 1946 American Canons, with its ambiguity, is clearly discernible here.[2]

The impediments to marriage listed in Schedule A are the prohibited degrees (including those 'normally prohibited by local or tribal custom'), mistake as to identity, lack of free and competent consent due to fraud, duress, mental deficiency or insanity, impotence or sexual perversion, and bigamy.

Those in whose favour a judgment has been given may be married in any church in the Diocese, or in another Diocese if the Bishop of that Diocese has approved the judgment. (Canon I. (d). ix.)

Canon II of the West African Marriage Canons provides for the operation of the Pauline Privilege in cases where one partner in a non-Christian marriage has received baptism and the non-Christian is 'unwilling to remain peacefully and without offence to God with the baptised partner without seeking to induce him/her to break any Christian law or prevent the baptism and Christian upbringing of the children'. As in the Indian Canons the Bishop is required to make a direct approach to the unbaptised partner so as to satisfy himself that such unwillingness exists.

Canon IV lays down that a communicant member of the Church who contracts a new union after divorce (other than in cases where the dissolved marriage is adjudged null) shall automatically be suspended from the reception of Holy Communion, but at the discretion of the Bishop he or she may be readmitted to Communion when the union has proved stable and after at least a year from the date of the remarriage.

2. On the American Canons see p. 40.

The 1967 Marriage Canons of the Church of the Province of East Africa follow the same general line as those of West Africa and are in large part verbally identical with them. There are, however, certain significant differences. Canon I, in defining the nature of marriage, lays emphasis on its indissolubility: marriage according to Christ's teaching is 'a lifelong, exclusive and indissoluble union and partnership, for better or for worse till death do them part, of one man and one woman to the exclusion of all others'. Canon II provides that no second marriage after divorce may be solemnised during the former partner's lifetime, and the only exception made is in the case of a civilly *annulled,* but not a civilly dissolved, marriage. In giving his judgment on a civilly annulled marriage the Bishop is required to have the concurrence of the majority of a panel of assessors constituted as in the West African Canon. The impediments to marriage are more fully defined than in the West African Canon, and included among them is the knowing and wilful acquiescence of the parties in a celebration of marriage lacking in proper legal formalities. Canon IV embodies the Pauline Privilege. Canon VII deals with discipline in the case of those who have remarried after divorce during the former partner's lifetime. A man so remarried, or one whose wife was previously married to a husband still living, shall not be eligible for Holy Orders or the office of Lay Reader. (Canon VII. 1). The Bishop has discretion to readmit remarried divorced persons to Communion. A period of a year must elapse, and the new union prove stable, before their readmission (Canon VII. 6).

The practice in the Province of Uganda is not yet the subject of a formal Canon, but it has been thus stated by the Archbishop:

> '(1) Those who have been married in church and subsequently obtain a divorce may not in any circumstances be remarried in church.
>
> (2) Where the marriage of a person who was married in church has clearly broken in such a way that there is very little hope of restoring it, then the Bishop may advise such a person to obtain a divorce through the Government Registry Office. A person who has obtained a divorce and has subsequently remarried (in a legally recognised manner, i.e. through a Registry Office) may then ask permission to remain a communicant. It is normal practice to allow a divorced person who has so remarried to have a Service of Blessing in church, and subject to the Bishop's permission, to remain a communicant.'

In the Church of England in Australia considerable differences exist between the dioceses in the matter of divorce and remarriage, which has not yet become the subject of regulation by the General Synod. In some dioceses it is the practice of the Bishop to give permission for the remarriage of divorced persons in church if they are church members in good standing, and if both parties sincerely desire the grace of God in their new marriage. This is the practice in the Diocese of Perth, where the present Archbishop has reverted to the practice followed prior to 1947 in the time of Archbishop Le Fanu.[3] The same procedure obtains in the dioceses of Bunbury, Gippsland, Grafton, Tasmania and Canberra-Goulburn. In the dioceses of Sydney and Armidale remarriage in church is allowed only in cases where the divorced person is the innocent party.

In the Province of Victoria, in the years following the last war, remarriage after divorce was allowed in church for an innocent party who was a regular communicant, but in 1957 the Bishops of the Province agreed that the marriage of no divorced persons in church should be permitted, except in cases where the first marriage was adjudged by the Diocesan Chancellor to be no true marriage in the eyes of the Church. Gippsland, however, as indicated above, is now an exception to this Provincial ruling.

In the dioceses of the Province of Queensland a strict line is followed, and no remarriage of a divorced person with a partner still living is allowed in church, except in cases in which a decree of anulment could have been obtained or in which for other reasons there appears to be no marriage-bond as recognised by the Church. Similarly in the extra-provincial diocese of Adelaide it is the rule that no clergyman holding the Bishop's licence may officiate at the marriage of a divorced person whose previous partner is still living.[4]

3. Between 1947 and 1963 no remarriage after divorce was permitted in the Diocese of Perth. Cf. the words of Archbishop Moline's Charge quoted in Winnett, *Divorce and Remarriage in Anglicanism,* p. 262.

4. Strong views on the subject have been expressed by the present Bishop of Adelaide, Dr. Thomas Reed. In a Pastoral Address delivered on 5th September, 1966, he referred to 'the chaos which is arising in the Church' due to 'the unilateral action which is being taken in Australia by certain bishops and priests with regard to the remarriage of divorced persons in some dioceses. If this continues the confusion which is at present growing in the minds of church people could reach scandalous proportions and could cause more and more members of the Church to cease to regard the Form of Solemnisation of Marriage in the Book of Common Prayer to have any real meaning whatever'. (*An Honourable Estate,* p. 6). The Bishop urges that the Church's Marriage Service should be

In the extra-provincial diocese of Willochra the position regarding remarriage is that each case must be referred to the Bishop for a decision. Applications for admission to Communion after remarriage must be submitted through the parish priest to the bishop, who will require evidence that the couple are conscious that they have committed a breach of the Church's rule, and also that they are sincerely desirous of making a Christian family life.

In the dioceses in which remarriage after divorce is not permitted in church, the Bishops are nevertheless willing to readmit those civilly remarried to Communion by the exercise of their pastoral discretion.

The whole subject of divorce and remarriage is being studied at the present time by the Australian bishops with a view to preparing a Canon for consideration by the General Synod in 1969.

In the Province of New Zealand no divorced person may be remarried in church during the former partner's lifetime, but admission to Communion after remarriage may be granted by the bishop.

The Provincial Synod of the West Indies held in 1949, when considering the Lambeth Conference Resolutions on Marriage, decided that the Bishop's discretion in the admission of divorced and remarried persons to Communion should not be exercised in the Province. (Special provision was made for reviewing cases which might be held to fall within the scope of nullity). This refusal of Communion, in addition to that of remarriage in church, meant that the Province of the West Indies had adopted a stricter marriage discipline than prevailed anywhere else in the Anglican Communion. In 1965, however, the decision of 1949 was rescinded, and the Bishops of the Province may now exercise their discretion in admitting to Communion those remarried after divorce.

The practice of the Protestant Episcopal Church in the United States as laid down in the 1946 Canons has attracted widespread

---

reserved for 'communicants who have been carefully prepared for marriage', (ibid. p. 9). The Bishop also says that the Church should re-examine her theology of marriage, and if her theology were found to need revision, to revise her practice correspondingly, but till then her present formularies should be adhered to. (ibid., p. 10). The Bishop accepts the Lambeth Conference recommendation concerning the admission of divorced persons to Communion. He also thinks that a Service of Blessing for remarried divorced persons is desirable, a blessing not upon the union but upon the two persons. Such a service should 'include an act of penitence for the failure of the former marriage, as is provided in the liturgical books of the Orthodox Church, together with an affirmation of intention to abide by the Church's standard of marriage for the future'. (ibid., p. 11).

attention, and it received a measure of approval from the Committee on the Church's Discipline in marriage of the 1948 Lambeth Conference, which said of the procedure embodied in these Canons that 'the impression so far gained is that it will meet a real need and increase people's respect for the Church and for marriage'. The principle underlying the procedure in question is that of bringing within the scope of nullity as many marriages as possible which have been civilly dissolved, so that the remarriage of the parties (subject to their being church members in good standing and intending a Christian marriage) may be solemnised with the blessing of the Church. Canon 17 lists the following impediments to marriage:

(1) Consanguinity;
(2) Mistake as to the identity of either party;
(3) Mental deficiency of either party sufficient to prevent the exercise of intelligent choice;
(4) Insanity of either party;
(5) Failure of either party to have reached the age of puberty;
(6) Impotence, sexual perversion, or the existence of venereal disease in either party undisclosed to the other;
(7) Facts which would make the proposed marriage bigamous;
(8) Concurrent contract inconsistent with the contract constituting canonical marriage;
(9) Attendant conditions: error as to the identity of either party, fraud, coercion or duress, or such defects of personality as to make competent or free consent impossible.

Canon 18 lays down that in the case of a dissolved marriage, if any of the impediments listed in the previous Canon can be 'shown to exist or to have existed which manifestly establish that no marriage-bond as the same is recognised by this Church exists', a declaration to that effect may be given, and the new marriage take place with the rites of the Church. The applicant in these cases has to state on the ground of which impediment he or she seeks a declaration as to his or her matrimonial status, and the application may be referred to the Bishop's Council of Advisers or Matrimonial Court. Some of the impediments are those long recognised in Canon Law, but others are new and capable of a wide interpretation, and the phrase 'to exist or to have existed' could be taken as allowing as grounds for nullity factors arising subsequently to the marriage - what has been called 'extended nullity' - though it could be presumed that they were latent at the time of the marriage. There are in fact differences in interpretation and practice between one diocese and another, some dioceses taking a strict line and others a laxer one.[5]

The influence of the 1946 American Canon is seen in Resolution 94 of the 1948 Lambeth Conference, which thus qualifies the prohibition of remarriage in church after divorce: 'unless it has been established that there exists no marriage-bond recognised by the Church'. It is also seen in the Canons of those Churches, that of the Province of West Africa or the Anglican Church of Canada, for instance, which provide means whereby cases of dissolved marriages can be examined to determine whether there was in fact a marriage-bond as recognised by the Church.

The General Synod of the Church of England in Canada (now the Anglican Church of Canada) enacted in 1905 a Canon (XXVII) forbidding the clergy to solemnise the marriage of any divorced person with a partner still living. This prohibition was included as a rubric in the Marriage Service of the Canadian Prayer Book and was retained in the revision of 1960. In 1943, 1946 and 1949 attempts were made to alter the Canon so as to allow the remarriage in church of at least the innocent party, but the difference of opinion in the General Synod prevented any action being taken.[6] In 1962 the Church's Commission on Marriage and Related Matters, which had been established as far back as 1943, was authorised to study a statement made by the Archbishop of British Columbia and endorsed by his Synod. This recommended that reconsideration should be given to the question of remarriage after divorce, and distinguished between two types of case. 'Some cases', the statement said, 'should be annulments rather than divorces', while in others 'some discretionary power should be given to responsible diocesan or provincial officials to deal with special and deserving applications'.[7] As a result of three years of study by the Commission the draft of a new and enlarged Canon on Marriage was

5. A 'liberal' interpretation of the Canon is given in Bishop James A. Pike's *A Time for Christian Candor,* Appendix A: 'Facts which would have been an impediment to a marriage had they arisen before the marriage may now serve as a basis for the declaration of the right to remarry even though they arose after the marriage began. This new basis for a favorable judgment is commonly called "extended nullity".' For a criticism of the 1946 Canons from the indissolubilist standpoint see E. B. Guerry, *The Historic Principle of the Indissolubility of Marriage.*

6. Winnett, *Divorce and Remarriage in Anglicanism,* pp. 253-4.

7. Article 'The Marriage Canon' by Dr. Charles Feilding in *The Canadian Churchman,* July-August, 1967.

submitted in 1965 to the General Synod, which gave it a first reading, and in a slightly amended form it was ratified by the General Synod in 1967. The voting on this occasion showed a decisive majority in favour of the more liberal procedure which the new Canon embodied, although three bishops, those of Caledonia, Moosonee and the Arctic recorded their votes against it.

The 1967 Canon[8] affirms in its preface that 'marriage is a lifelong union in faithful love, for better, for worse, to the exclusion of all others on either side' and that 'this union is established by God's grace when two duly qualified persons enter into a contract of marriage in which they declare their intention of fulfilling its purposes and exchange vows to be faithful to one another until they are separated by death'. Nevertheless it is recognised that not all marriages conform to this standard, and the New Testament itself had to take account of divorce. 'In Christ's name', says the preface, 'separated spouses were encouraged to seek reconciliation. In his name also divorce was forbidden though not without exception. In certain circumstances a believer already married to an unbeliever might be declared free from such a marriage-bond; in others, and here in the name of Christ, remarriage during the lifetime of a former spouse was described, with one exception, as an adulterous union'. Thus the Canon here qualifies the absolute indissolubility of marriage by reference to the Pauline Privilege and the Matthaean Exception.

Parts I and II of the Canon deal with the prerequisites for marriage and with the solemnisation of marriage. It is declared to be the duty of the clergy to provide such instruction for those seeking marriage that they may 'come to it with a Christian understanding of its purpose and may be encouraged to give effect with God's help to the vows they are preparing to make'. The parties, moreover, are to be 'encouraged' to sign a declaration setting forth the lifelong character of marriage and their intention of fulfilling its purposes, defined as 'the mutual fellowship, support and comfort of one another, the procreation (if it may be) and the nurture of children, and the creation of a relationship in which sexuality may serve personal fulfilment in a community of faithful love'. (Schedule A).

The more controversial sections of the Canon are those which deal with the Determination of Marital Status (Part III) and the Remarriage of a Divorced Person (Part IV). The section on the Determination of Marital Status follows the general line of the 1946 American Canons.

8. Extracts from this Canon are given in the Appendix to this chapter.

Certain conditions are laid down for a valid marriage, one of which is the free and voluntary consent of the parties, and factors are listed which are inconsistent with the presence of such consent. Among such factors are mental illness or defect, intoxication by alcohol or drugs, fear, coercion, abduction, concealment of such facts as venereal disease, pregnancy by another man, homosexuality or alcoholism, incapacity or refusal of consummation, and (in the case of marriages with non-Christians) lack of intention on the part of the non-Christian to fulfil conditions as to the Christian party's freedom of religion and the Christian upbringing of the children (III. 2 C, 1-9). In cases where a marriage has been civilly annulled or dissolved, or alleged to have been dissolved 'by an extra-judicial or non-judicial and non-legislative act or event',[9] a member of the Church, or one desiring to marry according to the Church's rites, may apply to the Ecclesiastical Matrimonial Commission for a declaration that the marriage ceremony did not result in a marriage under this Canon. The application and a statement of all the relevant facts are to be laid before the Commission, which, if satisfied that a marriage under the Canon does not exist and therefore does not constitute an impediment to a canonical marriage, shall issue a declaration to that effect. (III. 5). The procedure under this section of the Canon is concerned with nullity, though to avoid confusion with the civil process of nullity the words 'nullity' and 'annulment' are not used. If an essential constituent of marriage as understood by the Church was lacking, the Commission declares the fact, irrespective of whether the marriage was by civil process annulled or dissolved. It is noted, however, that in certain cases approbation may have the effect of validating the marriage. (III. 2. D). Application may also be made to the Commission for leave to presume a partner's death.

Part IV of the Canon deals with the Remarriage of a Divorced Per-

9. This is intended to cover the case of marriages dissolved in countries where the civil law makes no provision for either legislative or judicial dissolution of marriage, but there is provision for dissolution of marriage by executive action or registration of divorce or an act of the parties, or else divorce by one of these means is an alternative to judicial divorce. In Norway, for example, a divorce is not complete until perfected by executive action. In Formosa divorce may be effected by the parties giving notice of dissolution to the Registrar. In Egypt the marriages of Christians may now be dissolved in the Shar'iyah Court by *talaknama*, i.e. the public repudiation of the wife by the husband. A number of persons whose marriages have been dissolved by such non-judicial and non-legislative acts will be found among immigrants into Canada. (For this information grateful acknowledgement is made to Professor Stuart Ryan, of the Faculty of Law, Queen's University, Kingston, Ontario.)

son whose former partner is still living. Persons whose marriages have been dissolved by decree of a competent court, and who desire to remarry with the Church's rites during the lifetime of a former partner, may apply to the incumbent of the parish where it is intended that the marriage shall take place, and he after investigation will forward the application, with his report upon it, to the Ecclesiastical Matrimonial Commission (IV. B. 1). Among the facts concerning which the Commission must be satisfied before granting the application are the following: the gravity of the cause of the divorce, the efforts made at reconciliation, the arrangements made for the former wife's maintenance and for the care and education of any children, the prospects of the stability and happiness of the proposed marriage, and the applicants' understanding of, and intention to enter into, Christian marriage (IV. 2. A-I). Applicants are *required* (and not merely, as in other cases, encouraged) to sign the declaration that they intend a lifelong union. (Schedule C. 5). In cases where the Commission considers that the dissolved marriage did not constitute a marriage under the Canon it may make a declaration to that effect (IV. 4. C).

Part V deals with the admission of divorced and remarried persons to Communion, other than those remarried under the provisions of this Canon. Any such person desiring a ruling as to his or her communicant status may apply through the incumbent to the bishop, who shall have regard in his judgment both to the provisions of the Canon and to the spiritual welfare of the applicant.

Part VI lays down the composition and procedure of the Ecclesiastical Matrimonial Commission. A Commission must be set up in every diocese (or in certain circumstances, in a group of dioceses) under the presidency of the bishop or a priest appointed by him. The bishop must appoint as members of the Commission at least two communicant members of the Church, clerical or lay, male or female, and he may appoint others as consultants without vote. The Commission must contain, among its members or consultants, a qualified lawyer, an expert in Canon Law, and a person specially skilled in pastoral care. The decision of the Commission shall be that of a majority of its members, but the confirmation of the diocesan bishop is necessary before it becomes effective (VI. 1. A-G).

The Schedule on procedure (Schedule D) provides that the Commission may notify the other party to the marriage or purported marriage, in respect of which an application is made under Part III or

Part IV of the Canon, and any other person concerned, of the application, informing the person notified that he or she may submit evidence or make representations to the Commission. The Commission may also require proof of any fact to be made by statutory declaration or orally by affirmation, and it may also require the authentication of documents. An applicant may be represented or assisted by counsel or by a person skilled in Canon Law and pastoral care. A hearing may take place, should the Commission see fit, in the presence of the applicant and of the other party to the marriage, if the latter should attend. The Commission may also make a decision without a hearing if it considers a hearing unnecessary and none is asked for by the applicant.

To safeguard the consciences of the clergy it is laid down that 'the discretion of a minister to decline to solemnise any particular marriage shall not be abrogated by this Canon' (I. 11. D), but an amendment has been proposed, and may later come into force, by which the bishop may authorise the solemnisation of a marriage in a church other than that of the objecting minister.

The line of thought underlying Part IV of the new Canadian Canon was explained in a speech to the General Synod by Professor Stuart Ryan, Chancellor of the Diocese of Ontario and a member of the Church's Commission on Marriage and Related Matters. 'The Commission' said Professor Ryan, 'has examined the doctrine of indissolubility and has concluded that it is not well founded in our Lord's teaching as found in Holy Scripture or in the tradition of the Church, and is not valid theologically or otherwise'. Professor Ryan was careful to make it plain that the intention to enter into a lifelong union is an essential of Christian marriage, but some marriages, though entered into with this intention, do not prove to be lifelong. Marriages may in fact die. In Professor Ryan's words, 'they cease to be living partnerships and become dead, empty shells, a source of harm to the parties rather than of blessing'. Society can grant release from the bond of marriage in such cases, but the Church cannot do so as long as it is committed by its Canon Law to a doctrine of indissolubility. Of this doctrine and the practice based upon it Professor Ryan declared:

> 'I cannot believe that our Lord, whose word is the Gospel of mercy and forgiveness, and who bids us be merciful as our Father in heaven is merciful, could have intended such a harsh and unfor-

giving rule to govern his Church throughout the nineteen centuries that separate us from his time and throughout the generations that will come after us to the end of the age. I am compelled to conclude that those who have created a rule of absolute indissolubility out of our Lord's sayings have misunderstood him.'

This conclusion, according to Professor Ryan, is borne out by the history of the Church, for at no time has Christendom been unanimous in adhering to the doctrine of indissolubility, a doctrine which is 'western and mediaeval' rather than Catholic. The practice of the Eastern Churches and of the Reformed Churches in allowing remarriage has to be taken into account, and even under Roman Canon Law annulments have been granted which have been barely distinguishable from divorces. Speaking for the Commission, Professor Ryan said that the machinery and procedure which it recommended would 'prove workable, expeditious, inexpensive and more efficient than any other scheme that has come to our notice' and would enable the Church to 'offer to divorced persons who wish to remarry a ministry of healing and forgiveness'.[10]

The 1967 Canadian Canon represents the most radical approach so far adopted anywhere in the Anglican Communion to the problem of divorce and remarriage. It marks an unambiguous break with the doctrine of indissolubility and by implication recognises that a marriage may die otherwise than by the physical death of one of its partners. The Canon is drawn up with what may seem to some an excess of lawyer-like detail and precision:[11] nevertheless according to an authoritative opinion the process which it lays down 'is not even a pale imitation of a civil court: it is in essence a pastoral exercise which has the future good of the applicants as its main object'.[12] It may be said with confidence that the Canadian Canon will be carefully studied by the other Churches of the Anglican Communion and that its influence may well prove considerable in leading many of those Churches to adopt a similar if not identical procedure in dealing with cases of marriage breakdown.

10. 'The Purpose of Part IV' in *The Canadian Churchman,* October 1967, being the text of Professor Ryan's address to the General Synod.
11. The Canon with its Schedules forms a booklet of fourteen closely printed pages.
12. 'The Marriage Canon', by Dr. Charles Feilding in *The Canadian Churchman,* July-August 1967. Dr. Feilding is Professor of Moral and Pastoral Theology in Trinity College, Toronto, and Secretary of the Commission on Marriage and Related Matters.

Appendix to Chapter III.

EXTRACTS FROM THE 1967 CANADIAN CANON, (CANON XXVII), ON MARRIAGE IN THE CHURCH

Part III

DETERMINATION OF MARITAL STATUS UNDER THIS CANON

1 Definitions

(A) 'Marriage' as defined by this Canon means that union described in the Preface of this Canon and further described in a clause 2 of this Part. With respect to marriage so defined, a man and a woman may nevertheless, for reasons of age or health or other serious cause, agree to marry upon condition that there shall be no sexual intercourse between them permanently or for a limited time or from time to time.

(B) 'Commission' as used in this Canon means the Ecclesiastical Matrimonial Commission established under Part VI of this Canon, and the effect of a decision of a Commission shall be as stated in clause 6 of Part VI.

2 Conditions of Valid Marriage under this Canon

The question whether a purported marriage constituted a marriage as defined by this Canon, shall be determined by the Commission in accordance with the following principles:

(A) The parties to a marriage are not qualified for the purpose of this Canon to marry each other if:

(1) Either of them is under the age of 16 years except as provided in clause 4 of Part I of this Canon,[1]

(2) They are related to each other by blood or marriage within the prohibited degrees listed in the Table of Kindred and Affinity set out in clause 3 of Part I of this Canon,

(3) Either of them has gone through a ceremony of marriage with a person who is living at the time of the application, unless

(a) The previous ceremony of marriage has been found, as provided in this Part, by the Commission not to have been

1. A minister may solemnise the marriage of a person under sixteen only for sufficient cause and in accordance with the civil law, and subject to the bishop's direction.

a marriage as defined by this Canon and therefore not to be an impediment to marriage under the Canon Law of this Church, or

(B) The previous marriage has been found by the Commission to have been dissolved or terminated according to the civil law applicable thereto and permission to marry has been given by the Commission, as provided by Part IV of this Canon.

(B) The contract of marriage requires the free and voluntary consent of the parties to marry each other upon the terms set out in the Preface of this Canon, based upon adequate understanding by each of them of the nature of the union and of the mutual relations of husband and wife and of parents and children.

(C) Consent to marry is not present where:

(1) One of the parties is at the time of the contract of marriage incapable by reason of mental defect, mental illness, alcoholic intoxication, or the influence of a drug, of having the necessary understanding or giving the necessary consent.

(2) One of the parties has been induced to consent by duress, by coercion, or by fear.

(3) The woman gives consent after having been abducted and before being set free.

(4) One of the parties is at the time of the contract of marriage mistaken with respect to the nature of the contract or of the union, or with respect to the identity of the other party.

(5) One of the parties is at the time of the contract of marriage deceived by misrepresentation or concealment of facts seriously detrimental to the establishment of the contract including among other things misrepresentation or concealment of:

(a) Venereal disease,

(b) Addiction to drugs or alcohol,

(c) Pregnancy, except as a result of intercourse with the man,

(d) Addiction to homosexual practice, sadistic conduct, or other abnormal practice endangering the life or health of the other party.

(6) The marriage has been agreed to upon a condition which is illegal, impossible or contrary to the nature of the union, as defined in this Canon.

(7) The marriage is intended to be a sham or mere form.

(8) Either party is incapable of consummating or unreasonably refuses to consummate the marriage by sexual intercourse, subject to clause 1 (A) of this Part.

(9) One of the parties is not a Christian and there is a condition that the Christian party shall be entitled to adhere to and practice Christianity or to bring up any children of the union as Christians, and the non-Christian party assents to the condition without intending that it shall be satisfied.

(D) In the cases mentioned in sub-paragraphs (2) (3) (4) (5) and (9) hereof, the party coerced, mistaken or deceived or otherwise imposed upon may by an act of will approbate the marriage and continue to cohabit with the other party when free to cease cohabitation after being freed from coercion, fear or abduction or after learning of the mistake, deception, concealment or other circumstance constituting the defect. What constitutes approbation is a question of fact in each case. The effect of approbation for the purpose of this Canon is to validate the marriage.

(E) Nothing contained in this Canon shall authorise the solemnisation of a marriage known to the minister or either of the parties to be invalid by civil law.

3 Conditions Governing Application Regarding Canonical Status

(A) An application for declaration of marital status under this Canon may be made where the applicant has gone through a ceremony of marriage with a person living at the time of the application and it is alleged that the ceremony did not constitute a marriage as defined by this Canon and where the marriage or purported marriage

(1) Has been annulled or declared null and void or dissolved or otherwise terminated by a legislature or court, or

(2) Is alleged to have been dissolved or otherwise terminated according to the civil law properly applicable thereto, by an extra-judicial or non-judicial and non-legislative act or event.

(B) An application under this clause may be made by a person who has gone through a ceremony mentioned in sub-clause (A) of this clause and who is

(1) A member of this Church, or

(2) A person who desires to marry according to the rites of this Church.

(C) (1) An application under this clause not made in the course of or with a view to proceedings preliminary to a marriage shall be made to the incumbent of the parish or mission where the applicant resides or is accustomed to worship.

(2) An application under this clause made in the course of or with a view to proceedings preliminary to a marriage shall be made to the incumbent of the parish or mission where it is desired that the intended marriage be celebrated.

(3) The incumbent receiving the application shall investigate it to the best of his ability and forward the application, together with his report thereon, through the appropriate channels to the Commission having jurisdiction in the diocese.

4 Form of Application

(A) An application for declaration of marital status under clause 3 shall be made in writing and signed by the applicant and shall contain the information required by Schedule B.

(B) The application shall be accompanied by:

(1) A certificate of performance or registration of the ceremony issued by a competent authority,

(2) The original or a copy of the legislative act or the judgment or decree referred to in Schedule B paragraphs 9 and 10, and of any other document necessary for proof of any fact, and proof of its authenticity.

(3) Statements in writing verifying all other relevant facts not within the knowledge of the applicant signed by persons having knowledge of the facts.

(4) Where there has been no legislative act and no judgment or decree as above mentioned, a reasoned opinion in writing, signed by a person professionally qualified to give an opinion in respect of the law in question, verifying that the purported marriage has been dissolved or otherwise terminated.

5 Decision of Commission

On an application for declaration of marital status under clause 3 of this Part, the Commission, when all relevant facts have been proved to its satisfaction, shall determine whether the ceremony gone through by the applicant resulted in a marriage under this Canon. If the Commission determines that the ceremony did not result in a marriage under this Canon and if the Commission is satisfied that the marriage or purported marriage has been annulled or declared null and void or dissolved or otherwise terminated by a legislature or competent court, or has been dissolved or otherwise terminated by another act or event according to the law properly applicable thereto, and that no civil impediment to the marriage of the applicant exists, the Commission shall make a declaration that the ceremony in question did not result in a marriage under this Canon and therefore does not constitute an impediment to marriage under the Canon Law of this Church. In all other cases the Commission shall declare that impediment exists.

6 [Procedure in cases of application for presumption of death.]

Part IV
THE REMARRIAGE OF A DIVORCED PERSON WHOSE FORMER PARTNER IS STILL LIVING

1 Application for permission to Remarry according to the Rites of the Church

(A) An application for permission to marry each other according to the rites of this Church may be made by two persons, one or both of whom has or have gone through a ceremony or ceremonies of marriage with a person or persons now living not a party or parties to the application, if the prior marriage or marriages is or are not questioned under this Canon in the application but has or have been dissolved or terminated by a legislature or legislatures or a court or courts or by another act or acts or event or events according to the law or laws applicable thereto. Where a marriage or purported marriage has been annulled for a defect not mentioned in clause 2 of Part III of this Canon, and no defect mentioned in that clause is alleged in respect thereof, it shall be deemed for the purposes of this Canon to have been dissolved.

(B) The application shall be made to the incumbent of the parish or mission where it is desired that the intended marriage be celebrated. The incumbent shall investigate the application to the best of his ability and forward it together with his report thereon, through the appropriate channels, to the Ecclesiastical Matrimonial Commission established under Part VI of this Canon having jurisdiction in the diocese.

(C) The application shall be made in writing and signed by both applicants and shall contain the information required by Schedule C.

2 Permission to Remarry according to the Rites of the Church

Permission to marry according to the rites of this Church may be granted by the Commission to the applicants notwithstanding the marriage or marriages of either or both of them to another person or persons now living, if the Commission is satisfied that -

(A) Any prior marriage in question has been validly dissolved or terminated in accordance with the law properly applicable thereto,

(B) The causes which led to the dissolution or termination were sufficiently grave to justify application under this Part,

(C) The applicant concerned tried in good faith before dissolution to effect reconciliation with the other party,

(D) If prior marriages of both applicants have been dissolved, there are grounds for special assurance of the probable stability of the intended marriage,

(E) If the applicants have committed adultery with each other, there is good reason for permitting the marriage other than an intention to enter into a mere *pro forma* marriage to legitimate a child or children,

(F) If a former wife of the male applicant is living, adequate provision has been made according to his means for the former wife, or there is good reason why the applicant should not be required to make that provision,

(G) Proper provision has been made for the care, maintenance, education and advancement of minor, disabled or otherwise dependent children of any prior marriage,

(H) If the children of a prior marriage are to live with the applicants, there is a reasonable prospect that the family relationship will be satisfactory,

(I) The applicants understand the Christian Doctrine of Marriage as defined in this Canon, and intend to enter into such a marriage, and believe on reasonable grounds that they have the capacity to enter into and sustain the marriage during their joint lives.

3 Refusal of Permission

If permission is not granted, the Commission, subject to clause 4 (C) of this Part, shall dismiss the application which may not be renewed thereafter before any Commission unless further information is available.

4 Special Cases

(A) If the Commission is satisfied that efforts towards reconciliation between the parties to a former marriage would have been ineffective as a result of the fault of either party or for any other reason, the requirement of clause 2 (C) may be dispensed with.

(B) If either applicant has entered into two or more marriages that have been dissolved, the Commission shall not grant permission unless special circumstances justifying permission are proved.

(C) Notwithstanding the form of the application, if the Commission is of the opinion that a prior purported marriage of an applicant did not constitute a marriage as defined by this Canon, and the conditions of Part III clause 5 are satisfied, the Commission may make a declaration under that clause in respect of the marriage in question.

Part V
ADMISSION TO HOLY COMMUNION IN SPECIAL CASES

In every case where a person who has been remarried, except as provided above in this Canon, whose former and present partners are both living, desires a ruling with respect to admission to Holy Communion, the case must be referred by the incumbent to the bishop of the diocese for his judgment. In arriving at his judgment the bishop shall have due regard for the spiritual welfare of the petitioner as well as the provisions of this Canon. The bishop shall give his judgment in writing to both the incumbent and the petitioner.

Part VI
ECCLESIASTICAL MATRIMONIAL COMMISSION

1 Diocesan Commission

(A) Subject to the provision of clause 2 of this Part, there shall be in each diocese an Ecclesiastical Matrimonial Commission, hereinafter called the Commission, to deal with applications under this Canon.

(B) The president of the Commission shall be the diocesan bishop or a bishop or priest appointed by him. In a diocese in which no other president has been appointed, in the absence of the diocesan bishop from the diocese or during a vacancy of the see the administrator of the diocese shall be the president.

(C) The diocesan bishop shall appoint two or more communicant members of this Church, clerical or lay, male or female, to be members of the Commission, and may appoint other persons to be consultants without vote.

(D) At least one member of the Commission or a consultant should be engaged in or be qualified to engage in the practice or teaching of civil law in the province, territory or other jurisdiction or each of them, in which the Commission acts and at least one member or a consultant should have special skill and knowledge in canon law and at least one in pastoral care.

(E) The Commission may delegate to one or more members or consultants the investigation of any application or class of applications and of any matter or matters related thereto and of ascertaining any relevant facts and reporting thereon to the Commission, and may accept and act on any report or may take or require further investigation.

(F) The decision of a Commission in respect of an application shall be that of a majority of its members.

(G) Before becoming effective, the decision of the Commission shall require confirmation by the diocesan bishop or a bishop appointed by him for the purpose or, if the See is vacant, the metropolitan or a bishop appointed by him for the purpose.

(H) The diocesan bishop shall appoint an officer of the Commission who shall be known as the registrar and shall act as clerk and secretary of the Commission, to receive applications, conduct correspondence, give notices, attend hearings and deliberations in person or by deputy and keep minutes of proceedings, and engross and promulgate decisions and communicate each decision to the appropriate incumbent and the applicant or applicants and shall keep the records of the Commission in the diocesan offices.

2 Joint Commission

(A) With the consent of the metropolitan of the ecclesiastical province and of the diocesan synods of the dioceses concerned, the diocesan bishops of two or more dioceses may establish a Joint Commission to deal with all applications made thereafter within any of the dioceses concerned. If the dioceses are in different ecclesiastical provinces, the consent of the metropolitan of each province shall be required.

(B) The diocesan bishops of the dioceses concerned shall at the time of the meeting of each provincial synod involved or otherwise from time to time as required elect a bishop to be president of the Joint Commission or confirm the appointment of one already in office. If the jurisdiction of the Joint Commission extends into two ecclesiastical provinces, the bishops of the dioceses concerned shall arrange the election of a president among themselves.

(C) The president of a Joint Commission shall appoint the registrar from time to time during his term of office as president.

(D) While a Joint Commission is in existence, its composition, organisation, powers and procedure shall with all necessary changes be the same as those of a diocesan Commission, and no diocesan Commission within its jurisdiction shall act, provided that–

(1) The diocesan bishops of the dioceses concerned shall join in the appointment of members of and consultants to the Joint Commission,

(2) Applications shall be submitted by the appropriate incumbent to the diocesan secretary of each diocese concerned and forwarded by him to the registrar forthwith,

(3) After a decision in an application has been made and promulgated, the registrar shall forward the decision, together with the application and all related documents, to the diocesan secretary of the diocese in which it was made, who shall submit the decision for confirmation to the authority mentioned in clause 1 (G) of this Part. On obtaining the determination of that authority the secretary shall keep it with the application and accompanying documents in the diocesan records in a confidential manner, and communicate the decision to the appropriate incumbent and the applicant or applicants.

(E) The diocesan bishop of a diocese under a Joint Commission may with the consent of his diocesan synod and of the metropolitan of the province withdraw his diocese from the jurisdiction of the Joint Commission in respect of applications made after the withdrawal. On so doing he shall forthwith establish a diocesan Commission.

3 Jurisdiction of Commission

Applications under this Canon shall be either

(A) Applications for declaration of marital status, under Part III of this Canon, or

(B) Applications for permission to marry according to the rites of this Church, under Part IV of this Canon.

4 Procedure

The procedure followed by a Commission shall be governed by the provisions of Schedule D.

5 Avoidance of Delay

Each application shall be dealt with as expeditiously as possible.

6 Limitation of Jurisdiction

Every finding and determination of the Commission shall be and shall be expressly stated to be made solely for the purposes of this Canon and not for the purpose of performing any function of a civil court or other civil authority, and shall otherwise be confined to the findings and declaration, or granting or refusal of permission, necessary for disposing of the application in respect of which it is made.

Part VII

FORMS

Forms for use in the administration of this Canon may be authorised from time to time by the National Executive Council of the General Synod.

SCHEDULE A

DECLARATION

We, ... and . . . ., hereby declare that we intend to enter into marriage which we acknowledge to be a union in faithful love, to the exclusion of all others on either side, for better or for worse, until we are separated by death.

We undertake to prepare ourselves for the exchange of vows at our wedding, recognising that by this mutual exchange our union in marriage will be established.

We intend to strive thereafter to fulfil the purposes of marriage:

the mutual fellowship, support and comfort of one another, the procreation (if it may be) and the nurture of children, and the creation of a relationship in which sexuality may serve personal fulfilment in a community of faithful love.

SCHEDULE B

APPLICATION FOR DECLARATION OF MARITAL STATUS

The following information must be provided so far as it is known:

1 The full name, and place of residence of the applicant,

2 The date and place of the marriage ceremony in question, its nature and form, by or before whom it was celebrated or solemnised, and the authority or purported authority of the celebrant,

3 The full name, and the place of residence if known, of the other party to the ceremony at the time of the application,

4 The ages of the parties at the time of the ceremony, their then respective places of residence, domiciles and nationalities, their relationships toward each other by blood or marriage, whether either of them was under any disability or prohibition with respect to marriage generally or with respect to the other party, and the respective marital conditions of the parties immediately before the ceremony,

5 The proper law applicable to the ceremony and to the marriage otherwise than with reference to the ceremony, the relevant provision of the proper law or laws and authorities for such provisions,

6 Whether the requirements of the proper law or law with respect to banns, licence or permit, to consent of parents or others, to examinations and other preliminary matters were duly complied with,

7 The alleged defects in the ceremony or in the marriage or purported marriage,

8 Whether (if relevant) either party has exercised any legal right to avoid the marriage or purported marriage or has approbated the marriage,

9 Full particulars of any proceedings in any court or ecclesiastical tribunal or commission in which the validity of the marriage or purported marriage was questioned directly or indirectly and the result of such proceedings,

10 Full particulars of any proceedings in any court or legislature or of any other act or event by which the marriage or purported marriage was or is alleged to have been dissolved or terminated,

11 Whether there have been children of the marriage or purported marriage and, if so, the full name, age, place of residence and present marital status of each child now living,

12 If any child of the marriage or purported marriage is a minor or under any disability or otherwise dependent on one or both of the parties to the marriage or purported marriage a statement showing who has the custody or is directly or indirectly responsible for the care and maintenance of the child and full details of present financial and other arrangements and future plans for the care, maintenance, education, and advancement of the child,

13 Where a male applicant has been a party to a ceremony of marriage with a woman now living, a statement showing what provision has been made and is being carried out for the present and future maintenance of the former wife or purported wife, or an explanation why there is no such provision,

14 Any other facts that would assist the Commission.

SCHEDULE C

APPLICATION FOR PERMISSION TO REMARRY ACCORDING TO THE RITES OF THE CHURCH

The following is required:

1 The information with respect to any prior marriage of either applicant with a person now living mentioned in Schedule B paragraphs 1, 2, 3, 4, 9, 10, 11, 12, 13, and 14.

2 A full explanation of the cause of the breakdown of the former marriage and the cause or grounds of dissolution or termination and of all efforts towards reconciliation and an explanation why no other efforts towards reconciliation were made,

3 A statement setting out the negotiations, if any, between the parties to the former marriage leading up to dissolution or termination,

4 Information necessary to enable the Commission to determine any question that must be determined under clause 2 of Part IV,

5 The Declaration set out in Schedule A, signed by both applicants,
6 Particulars of any previous application under Part IV made to any Ecclesiastical Matrimonial Commission.

SCHEDULE D

PROCEDURE OF THE COMMISSION

1 Unless a marriage or purported marriage in respect of which an application is made has been civilly annulled or declared null and void or dissolved or terminated by a competent legislature or a competent court at the instance of or after due notice to the party thereto other than the applicant herein, the Commission shall before making a finding or determination cause the other party to be notified of the application in a manner that satisfies the Commission that the notice has been brought to the attention of the other party, if it is feasible to give such notice.
2 In any case the Commission may cause the other party to the marriage or purported marriage, or any other person whom the Commission believes to be concerned, to be notified of the application, if notification is feasible.
3 The notice shall be accompanied by a copy of the application and shall inform the person notified that he or she may assert or dispute any statement of fact, submit evidence orally or in writing and make any submission or representation he or she sees fit to make in person or by representative.
4 Any statement, dispute, evidence, submission or representation made in response to the notice shall be communicated to the applicant who shall be given an opportunity of making answer or rebuttal.

The Commission may:

5 Require proof of any additional fact which appears to be relevant to the matters involved in the application,
6 Require proof of any fact to be made by statutory declaration or to be made orally by affirmation, and require any document to be satisfactorily authenticated,
7 Require the applicant, in order to remove doubt, to take such proceedings in a competent civil court as may be necessary to establish or confirm the nullity of any purported marriage not

already annulled or declared null and void by a court or legislature or the dissolution or termination of any marriage not dissolved or terminated by a court or legislature, or the competence in the premises of any court or legislature whose act, judgment or decree is relied on in relation to the marital status of the applicant,

8 Permit an application to be represented or assisted by counsel or by a person having special skill and knowledge in canon law and pastoral care,

9 Make findings of fact based on any evidence satisfactory to the Commission submitted in a manner satisfactory to the Commission, whether written or oral and direct or hearsay and whether or not verified by oath, affirmation or statutory declaration,

10 Conduct a hearing, if the Commission sees fit, in the presence of the applicant and of the other party to a marriage or purported marriage, if the other party desires to attend, and of their representatives or assistants, or make a determination without a hearing if the Commission does not consider a hearing to be necessary, and no application for a hearing is made by the applicant,

11 Permit an application to be reopened or a fresh application to be made if further information is available after the Commission has disposed of an application.

IV

DIVORCE AND REMARRIAGE: THE ECUMENICAL CONTEXT

Discussions concerning Christian reunion have been for the most part concerned with questions relating to the Church, the ministry and the sacraments, and little attention has been paid to difference of views concerning the doctrine and discipline of marriage. Nevertheless at some stage the attempt would have to be made to reach a common mind and a common practice in a matter which touches so closely the life of the ordinary church member.[1] In the Interim Statement of the Anglican-Methodist Unity Commission, *Towards Reconciliation,* marriage discipline was put forward from both the Anglican and the Methodist side as one of the subjects which would have to be considered by the Commission before Stage One of the proposed scheme of union could be implemented.[2] In this chapter a survey will be made of the teaching and practice in the matter of divorce and remarriage of the major Christian bodies other than the Anglican Communion.

From early times, at least from the sixth century, differing views have been held within Christendom concerning the indissolubility of the marriage-bond, the Western Church in general holding a validly contracted and consummated marriage to be indissoluble absolutely, and the Eastern Church regarding marriage as in ideal and intention indissoluble yet capable of dissolution for certain grave causes.

The divorce law of the Eastern Orthodox Churches corresponds in the main with the 117th Novel of Justinian and permits divorce for

1. 'In any consideration of reunion it will be necessary to face seriously the differing marriage disciplines of the various Churches, and to determine how far the demand that there must be one uniform practice in every Church and in every country can be maintained.' Bishop A. M. Hollis, 'Anglicanism and Unity' in *Essays in Anglican Self-Criticism,* (edited by D. M. Paton), p. 219.

2. *Towards Reconciliation,* pp. 77-78. While this book is passing through the press the Final Report of the Anglican-Methodist Unity Commission has been published. The Commission recognises that differences in marriage discipline cannot be immediately resolved and recommends that in cases where an Anglican seeks to be remarried after divorce an application for marriage in a Methodist Church should be refused, subject to the following exception: 'Where the proposed marriage is between an Anglican and a person who owns allegiance to the Methodist Church, it would not, in our opinion, be a breach of the pledge if, after carrying out requirements laid down in the Methodist discipline and in consultation with his Church of England colleague, the Methodist Minister agreed to solemnise the marriage.' *Anglican-Methodist Unity (2) The Scheme* pp. 85-86.

the following causes: adultery and conduct giving rise to suspicion of adultery, high treason, attempt by one on the life of the other, intentional commission of abortion by the wife, desertion, prolonged disappearance and impotence continuing for three years.[3] Insanity, leprosy and irreconcilable hatred were classed by Archbishop Germanos as 'grounds which are to be found in the sources of civil law but have not been accepted by the Church',[4] yet in fact the Orthodox Churches have at times granted divorces on these grounds.[5] Remarriage after divorce is allowed, but no marriage beyond the third is permissible. All second marriages, including those of widowers and widows, are regarded as falling short of the highest and to that extent they are tolerated rather than positively approved, and this is reflected in the form of service prescribed for marriages after the first.[6] In Greece the civil courts exercise jurisdiction in divorce, but first the bishop must attempt reconciliation, and the granting of the decree is followed by the granting of the ecclesiastical document of divorce,[7]

Though the Eastern Churches have accorded a respect to the law of a Christian state side by side with that of the Canons, Orthodox theologians repudiate the notion that Orthodox practice represents an accommodation to the law of the state. Rather they would justify it on theological grounds, as for example when Professor Alivisatos says that marriage can be dissolved by 'moral death', that is, 'by causes defeating entirely the very end and scope of marriage'.[8] The permission of remarriage after divorce is a concession to human weakness or the 'hardness of men's hearts', which falls within the exercise of 'economy', or the Church's relaxation of the full strictness of its laws with a view to the ultimate salvation of its members. Thus, according to Professor Alivisatos, the Church's practice aims 'at the success of the end purpose of the Church, which is the endeavour of the final salvation pursued "in season and out of season", in

3. Lacey-Mortimer, *Marriage in Church and State,* pp. 108-9; H. S. Alivisatos, *Marriage and Divorce in accordance with the Canon Law of the Orthodox Church,* pp. 14-15.
4. Appendix II, 'The Doctrine and Discipline of the Orthodox Church with reference to Divorce', in Report of the Joint Committees of the Convocations, *The Church and Marriage,* (1935), pp. 56-57.
5. G. H. Joyce, *Christian Marriage,* pp. 373-5.
6. *Service Book of the Holy Orthodox Catholic Apostolic Church* (edited by I. F. Hapgood) pp. 293-305.
7. Appendix II *The Church and Marriage,* p. 57.
8. Alivisatos, op. cit., p. 12.

order that it, the Church, "made all things to all men, might be able by all means to save some" '.[9]

As is well known, the Roman Catholic Church maintains the doctrine of absolute indissolubility, at least in respect of the consummated marriages of Christians. The unconsummated marriage of Christians is capable of dissolution by Papal dispensation or by the taking of solemn religious vows by one of the partners. Roman Canon Law provides for the operation of the Pauline Privilege in the cases of the marriages of converts, but certain Papal decisions would appear to give a wider interpretation to the Privilege than that envisaged by the Apostle. So G. H. Joyce writes: 'There are circumstances in which the road to heaven would present extreme difficulty to the convert, if dissolution were impossible . . . Here the Pope can intervene *in favorem fidei* and sever a bond which lacks the absolute indissolubility proper to a consummated marriage between the baptised'.[10] Otherwise marriage is incapable of dissolution, and Canon Seven of the *Canones de Sacramento Matrimonii* of the Council of Trent, which Joyce calls 'a dogmatic definition of the indissolubility of marriage',[11] reads as follows:

> 'If anyone shall say that the Church is in error when it taught and still teaches, in accordance with the teaching of the Gospels and the Apostles, that the bond of marriage cannot be dissolved by reason of the adultery of one of the partners, and that neither of them, not even the innocent one who gave no cause to the adultery, can contract another marriage while the other partner is alive, and that the man who dismisses his adulterous wife and marries another, and the woman who dismisses her adulterous husband and marries another, are guilty of adultery - let him be anathema.'[12]

Among non-Roman Catholics there exists the suspicion that the Roman Church today, like the later mediaeval Church, uses the procedure of annulment to bring about what is in effect the dissolution of a marriage. This suspicion may be unjustified,[13] though it is true that the Church is in a position in many cases to declare null and void

9. Ibid., p. 18. On the Orthodox teaching on divorce and remarriage see also Timothy Ware, *The Orthodox Church,* pp. 301-2.
10. Joyce, *Christian Marriage,* p. 497.
11. Ibid., p. 395.
12. Ibid., p. 392: The Latin text will be found on p. 613.
13. For an exposition and defence of Roman Catholic practice in the matter of nullity see F. J. Sheed, *Nullity of Marriage.*

marriages which have been civilly dissolved, thus enabling a second marriage to be solemnised with Roman Catholic rites. The *Ne Temere* decree (following the chapter *Tametsi* of the Council of Trent) makes the presence of the parish priest or his delegate essential to the valid marriage of a Roman Catholic. As all those who have received baptism in the Roman Catholic Church, even though they have been brought up outside the Church or have never practised their religion, are subject to the Church's jurisdiction, a non-practising Roman Catholic who marries in an Anglican church or a register-office is not validly married in the eyes of the Church, and this marriage if dissolved by a decree of divorce is no obstacle to marriage with a second partner by the rites of the Church.

The reconsideration of beliefs and practices long held to be authoritative in respect of certain ethical questions, which is now taking place in the Roman Catholic Church, and of which the debate on contraception is the outstanding example, has extended to marriage and divorce. At the Fourth Session of the Second Vatican Council, in September 1965, Archbishop Zoghby, Patriarchal Vicar of the Melchites in Egypt, urged that in cases of adultery or desertion the Church should grant a divorce allowing the innocent party to remarry. The alternative, lifelong continence, demanded a heroic virtue which could not be imposed upon all.[14] Another bishop who has expressed himself in similar terms is Dr. Francis Simons, Bishop of Indore, the bishop who in the discussion on contraception at the Vatican Council declared, 'Laws, even the natural law, are for men, not men for laws'. In an article Dr. Simons has written: 'Jesus told the scribes that Moses had allowed divorce and remarriage because of the hardness of his people's hearts, but do we not also have today a number of people who find it impossible to make a success of a marriage, or to live a continent life once their marriage has broken up?'[15]

A radical call to the Roman Church to reconsider its position on divorce and remarriage has been sounded by Fr. Victor Pospishil, a priest of the Byzantine Rite in the United States, in his book, *Divorce and Remarriage: Towards a New Catholic Teaching.* The author recognises that there are cases of marriage breakdown for which divorce provides the only remedy, and that the denial of divorce en-

14. Xavier Rynne, *The Fourth Session,* pp. 83-85.
15. 'The Catholic Church and the New Morality', *Cross Currents,* Vol. XVI, No. 4, quoted in Pospishil, *Divorce and Remarriage: Towards a New Catholic Teaching,* p. 105.

tails suffering for vast numbers of faithful Catholics, as well as causing many of them to live in irregular unions. The answer lies, according to Fr. Pospishil, in the use by the Church of the 'power of the keys', entrusted to her by Christ, to loose as well as to bind partners in marriage, and when marriage is so dissolved by properly constituted authority in the Church it is not man but God who puts asunder.[16] The Papal dissolution of non-consummated marriages, the practice of the Eastern Churches, and the concessions made in certain early Penitentials and decrees of synods are cited as precedents for the course which the author is advocating.[17]

A further example of fresh thinking in the Roman Catholic Church on the subject of marriage is afforded by Dr. J. Dominian, a psychiatrist, in an article 'Vatican II and Marriage' in *The Clergy Review* for January 1967. Referring to the numbers each year of people whose marriages end in divorce, Dr. Dominian asks, 'Are all these people breaking God's law?' If we have thought so, it is because (to quote his words) 'we have worked on the belief that in the absence of any of the usual impediments a man validly married. Verbal consent, freely given, constitutes marriage'. But as a psychiatrist Dr. Dominian believes that it is necessary to re-examine the criteria of a valid marriage, and he writes thus in his article:

> 'Men and women can certainly give and receive each other's verbal vows to take each other in marriage. What has to be established is that they are physically and psychologically capable of effecting a minimum expression of what these vows signify . . . . . The Church has always recognised the minimum requirement of physical consummation without which separation and remarriage is possible. Today we are beginning to recognise this minimum requirement in psychological terms.'[18]

16. V. J. Pospishil, *Divorce and Remarriage: Towards a New Catholic Teaching*, pp. 126 ff.
17. These are discussed by Fr. Pospishil in a long appendix, pp. 141-200.
18. *The Clergy Review,* January 1967, p. 26. The February 17th, 1968, issue of *America,* a periodical published by the Jesuit Order in the United States, contained four articles on 'The Reform of Canon Law concerning Marriage, Annulment and Divorce', in which strong criticism is expressed of existing procedure. According to Fr. J. R Hertel it has 'institutionalised what in a real-life situation can only be personalised'. Dr J. T. Catoir, a Presiding Judge of a Diocesan Matrimonial Tribunal argues that 'a genuine love commitment' is essential to a sacramental, and therefore, indissoluble marriage. Where this is absent dissolution should be allowed, and the proof needed 'would not depend on an

From this Dr. Dominian draws the conclusion that marriages may fulfil all the canonical requirements and yet not be true marriages owing to the presence of psychological immaturity or defects which prevent even the minimal expression of married love. Such marriages should presumably, in Dr. Dominian's view, be capable of annulment or dissolution.

The foregoing are only expressions of individual opinion within the Roman Catholic Church, and they have not yet affected the official doctrine and practice of the Church. Sooner or later, however, the rethinking of the whole subject of marriage which is taking place in the Roman Communion may well lead to a revision of past attitudes and traditional positions. In view of the recent rapprochement between the Roman Catholic and the Eastern Orthodox Churches the question may be asked whether a difference of practice in the matter of divorce and remarriage would be an obstacle to union if agreement were reached on other matters. The precedent of the Council of Florence in the fifteenth century suggests that it might not. The question of divorce and remarriage was not included among the points of difference to be discussed at the Council, and it was only after agreement had been reached that Pope Eugenius called on the Eastern bishops to change their practice regarding divorce, and when the latter demurred the matter was not pressed. The Pope was not prepared to jeopardise the union for the sake of securing uniformity in respect of marriage and divorce.[19]

The Protestant Reformers of the sixteenth century were almost unanimously in favour of divorce for adultery and desertion, with the right of remarriage at least for the innocent party, and their view found expression in the practice of the Reformed Church on the Continent and in Scotland. In Scotland from the time of the Reformation onwards divorce was permitted both by Church law and by civil law for adultery and desertion, but restrictions were placed on remarriage, in that a law of the Church of Scotland passed in 1566 forbade the marriage of guilty parties, and an Act of the Scottish

19. E. I. Watkin, *The Church in Council,* p. 172.

---

investigation of the obscure and remote actions and intentions that existed prior to the contract: it would depend on the easily verifiable behaviour pattern that followed the marriage'. (I am grateful to Dr Rosemary Lauer for bringing these articles to my notice).

Parliament in 1600 forbade the marriage of paramours.[20] Until recently ministers of the Church of Scotland were prohibited from officiating at the marriage of guilty parties, but the whole question of the remarriage of divorced persons was the subject of two reports submitted to the General Assembly in 1959. After considerable debate in the Assembly an *Act of the Marriage of Divorced Persons* was passed, giving ministers the liberty of marrying, subject to certain conditions, not only innocent, but also repentant guilty, parties. The terms of the Act are here given in full:

'(1) A Minister of the Church of Scotland may lawfully solemnise the marriage of a person whose former marriage has been dissolved by divorce and whose former spouse is still alive, provided that the said Minister adhere to the requirements stated hereunder.

(2) A Minister shall not accede as a matter of routine to a request for the solemnisation of marriage of persons whose marriage has been dissolved by a decree of divorce as aforesaid.

(3) A Minister invited to celebrate such a second marriage shall, in order to enable him to make his decision, take all reasonable steps to obtain relevant information, which shall normally include the following:

(a) adequate information concerning the life and character of the parties to be married; here the very greatest caution shall be exercised in cases where for any reason no pastoral relationship exists between the Minister and either or both of the parties concerned;

(b) the grounds and circumstances of the divorce case;

(c) facts bearing upon the future well-being of any children concerned;

(d) whether any other Minister of Religion has declined to solemnise the proposed remarriage;

(e) the denomination to which the parties belong: special care shall be taken in cases where one of both parties belong to a denomination whose discipline on this matter may differ from the Church of Scotland.

(4) A Minister shall also consider whether there is any danger of scandal arising if he solemnise the remarriage; at the same time he shall take into careful consideration, before refusing to solemnise

20. 'Statement on Marriage and Divorce in Scotland', by Dr. A. P. Sym, Appendix III, in Report of the Joint Committees of the Convocations, *The Church and Marriage*, (1935).

the remarriage, the moral and spiritual effect of his refusal on the parties seeking such a marriage.

(5) As the determinative factor, a Minister shall do all he can to assure himself that by word and deed there has been sincere repentance where guilt has existed in the past on the part of any divorced person seeking remarriage. He shall also give the most careful instruction, where this is needed, in the nature and requirements of a Christian marriage.

(6) A Minister shall not be required to solemnise a remarriage against his conscience.

(7) Every Presbytery shall appoint certain individuals (who need not be members of the Presbytery concerned) with one of whom Ministers in doubt as to the correct course of action may consult if they so desire: in such cases the final decision must rest with the Minister who has been asked to officiate.

(8) A Minister shall submit annually to the Presbytery a return of the number of divorced persons who have been parties to marriages solemnised by him by virtue of this Act. Such return shall contain no details beyond the number of such persons.

(9) The admission to Communion of persons who have contracted marriage after divorce, and any other matters affecting pastoral care, shall remain the responsibility of the Minister and Kirk Session involved'.[21]

The General Assembly of the Presbyterian Church of England in 1946 gave the following direction to ministers on the subject of the remarriage of divorced persons:

> 'The Assembly respects the view of those who believe the marriage of divorced persons to be contrary to New Testament teaching, and instructs its ministers who do not adhere to this strict view to conduct such marriages only when they are satisfied either:
>
> (a) that the person seeking marriage was morally innocent in the divorce, or
>
> (b) that the divorced person has expressed penitence and has been admitted, or readmitted, to the Christian Church.'

In subsequent years, however, the desire gained ground for a revision of this instruction, and the matter came four times before the General Assembly. In 1964 a motion was brought before the General Assem-

21. J. T. Cox and J. B. Longmuir, *Practice and Procedure of the Church of Scotland* (5th edition, 1964) pp. 56-58.

bly to rescind the 1946 instruction and to require ministers to examine the circumstances of each application for remarriage before reaching a decision. This motion was not carried, but instead the Church and Community Committee of the Assembly was requested to continue its study of the question. As the result of their report the General Assembly of 1967 rescinded the instruction of 1946 and replaced it by the following:

'(A) The Assembly authorises ministers, after serious consideration of the issues involved and when confident that it is right to do so, to solemnise the remarriage of a divorced person.

(B) The Assembly instructs ministers, when preparing such a person for remarriage, to discharge their pastoral responsibility in such a way as to help that person and future partner to build up a truly Christian marriage within the life of the Church.

(C) The Assembly requests ministers, in cases of exceptional difficulty in deciding upon an application for remarriage, to consult privately either another minister or one or two members of Session.

(D) The Assembly declares that no minister shall be required to solemnise a remarriage against his conscience.'

The Presbyterian Church of Wales issued in 1949 a *Declaration on Marriage and Divorce,* part of which reads as follows:

'We recognise that marriage itself, except in ideal, is not absolutely indissoluble. When divorce has been granted by a British Court of Law we accept the fact that the marriage has been dissolved, and that the divorced persons are free to remarry . . . . . . When a minister is asked to remarry a divorced person who is a member of the Church under his care, he should satisfy himself that the person seeking remarriage was an innocent party or is truly repentant. Then if he judges from personal knowledge of the bride and bridegroom that they are proper persons for him to officiate at their marriage, the Church permits him to do so after consultation with his elders. Every Presbytery should appoint a committee of three suitable persons whom a minister might consult in such a matter should he feel the need for doing so . . . . . . The Church does not lay upon any minister the duty of officiating at the marriage of divorced persons, if to do so would be against his own judgment and that of his elders.'

The 1948 Code of the Presbyterian Church of Ireland contains this recommendation concerning the remarriage of divorced persons:

> 'While this Church does not prohibit the marriage of a divorced person or persons, it is strongly recommended that ministers do not join in marriage the guilty party in a divorce suit, except in circumstances recognised by the Moderator's Advisory Committee as justifying such action.'[22]

The Congregational Church (formerly the Congregational Union) in England and Wales allows freedom to its ministers in the matter of solemnising marriages of the divorced, but guidance was provided in the report, published in 1953, of a Commission appointed by the Congregational Union to consider the question. This report is one of the ablest documents of its kind, as would be expected from a Commission which numbered among its members two such leading theologians as Dr. Nathaniel Micklem and the late Principal Sidney Cave. The Commission, after reviewing the teaching of the New Testament, reached the conclusion that 'lifelong fidelity in marriage is alone in accordance with the divine will', yet 'the hardness of heart to which our Lord referred still remains' and 'marriages are indissoluble in the sense that they should not be dissolved: they are not indissoluble in the sense that they cannot be'.[23]

The report distinguishes three classes of divorced persons who may seek to be remarried in a Congregational Church: they may be (a) members of a Congregational Church; or (b) members of a Church which on principle declines to perform of the ceremony; or (c) associated with no Church except in some vague way. With regard to (a), the recommendation is that only a genuinely innocent party or one who is truly repentant should be permitted to remarry in a Congregational Church (though two members of the Commission held that no guilty party should be so remarried during the lifetime of the other party). But even in cases where a marriage in church would be inappropriate, it must be recognised that the remarriage may be the best course possible under the circumstances and therefore right: on this the Commission observes, 'It may seem illogical that we should argue

22. Paragraph 261. The functions of the Moderator's Advisory Committee are defined in paragraph 452 as 'to give to the Moderator of the General Assembly counsel on matters of importance regarding which he desires to have advice, and thus, as far as possible, to relieve him of responsibility when he is doubtful as to what his decision should be'. In 1966 the Moderator's Advisory Committee was incorporated into the General Board of Assembly.
23. *Report of the Commission on the Marriage of Divorced Persons*, p. 12.

on the one hand that the ceremony may not properly be performed in church and on the other that the remarriage may under certain circumstances be approved, but we are bound as Christians both to maintain the sanctity of the vows taken in church and at the same time to recognise moral possibilities and impossibilities'.[24]

Under class (b) come the numerous cases of Anglicans who turn to a Congregational Church because their own Church has refused them remarriage. Here the general principle is laid down, that 'it is not the duty of Congregational ministers actively to assist members of other denominations to break the rules of their own Church'. Nevertheless exceptions may be made in the cases of Anglicans who are such merely in name and of those who have in effect broken with Anglicanism and are prepared to seek admission to a Congregational Church.

With regard to class (c), those unassociated, or only vaguely associated, with any Church may be remarried in a Congregational Church 'if they seriously intend to live in the fellowship of the Church, and wherever they may be, to subject themselves to pastoral oversight'.[25]

The Commission finally emphasises the necessity for agreement between minister and Church Meeting on the question of the remarriage of divorced people.[26]

The Baptists, like the Congregationalists, uphold the freedom of individual churches and ministers make their own responsible decisions, and therefore in the matter of remarriage after divorce the Baptist Union has offered only general guidance. The Council of the Union discussed the question in 1951 and came to the conclusion that there was no objection to the remarriage of divorced persons in a Baptist Church when there was a genuine desire to start afresh. In cases of doubt a minister was advised to consult with his deacons or Area Superintendent.[27]

A Statement on Marriage and Divorce adopted by the Methodist Conference in 1946 affirmed that Jesus, in spite of certain ambiguities

24. Ibid., p. 19.
25. Ibid., p. 20.
26. Ibid., p. 21.
27. *Home and Family Life: a Statement prepared by the Citizenship Committee of the Baptist Union,* Section 6. The Secretary of the Baptist Christian Citizenship Committee, Mr J. E. T. Hough, writes: 'No Baptist minister who consents to remarry in church persons who have been divorced will do so without first enquiring exhaustively into all the circumstances which led to the divorce in question. The fact remains that ideally all Christians regard Christian marriage as a lifelong monogamous union which death alone may break.' *Adventures in Christian Obedience,* p. 40.

in his recorded teaching, recalled men to the divine principle of lifelong marriage, but left it 'to the reason and conscience of his disciples, under the guidance of the Holy Spirit, to interpret and apply that principle to every condition and age'.[28] The fact of marriage breakdown must be realistically faced, but divorce is only justified when the marriage has broken down beyond the power of restoration.[29]

Earlier, in 1935, the Methodist Conference, replying to questions from two Overseas Districts, ruled that a member of the Methodist Church who is an innocent party in a case of adultery is permitted to sue for divorce, and that a member who is an innocent party in an action in which a divorce has been granted may marry again.[30]

The Conference of 1945 drew up regulations regarding the membership in the Methodist Church of those who had been parties to divorce proceedings whether as petitioner, respondent or co-respondent. It was ordered that the Leaders' Meeting should consider the question of their continuance in membership before referring the case to the District Discipline Committee, whose decision should be communicated to the Leaders' Meeting, with a provision for reference to Conference in the event of disagreement between the Leaders' Meeting and the District Discipline Committee. The District Discipline Committee was empowered to reinstate those removed from membership if it 'is satisfied that the person concerned is sincerely penitent and has made, or is prepared to make, such reparation as may be possible'.[31]

The remarriage of divorced persons in a Methodist Church is governed by the following regulation made by Conference in 1948:

> 'If a request is made by any person whose previous marriage has been dissolved, whether such a person is a member of the Methodist Church or not, to be married in a Methodist Church or by a Methodist Minister elsewhere, or should a civil marriage already have been contracted by any such person and a request made that a religious service in a Methodist Church may follow such a marriage, the request shall be considered by the Minister concerned after he has interviewed both parties. Every endeavour must be made to uphold the principles and ideals embodied in the Con-

28. *Statement of the Methodist Church concerning the Law of Marriage and Divorce,* p. 3.
29. Ibid., p. 5.
30. *Minutes of Conference 1935,* Standing Order 109, p. 285.
31. *Minutes of Conference 1945,* quoted in *Statement etc.* pp. 6 and 7.

ference Statement on Divorce and the Conference Declaration on the Christian View of Marriage and the Family. Should the Minister be in any doubt as to the proper course to take, he shall refer the matter to the Ministers of the Circuit, who in their turn may refer any case about which there is doubt to a special Committee called together at the discretion of the Chairman of the District. Those other than Ministers in Full Connection with the Conference who may be requested to officiate at such marriages shall act under the direction of the Superintendent of the Circuit. In all cases the Minister shall consult the Chairman of the District before the ceremony takes place. Under no circumstances does the Conference require a Minister to officiate at the marriage of a divorced person should it be contrary to the dictates of his conscience to do so.'[32]

The British Provincial Synod of the Moravian Church (Unitas Fratrum) drew up in 1937, and reaffirmed in 1956, the following Statement on Marriage and Divorce:

> 'The Church upholds for all the ideal of Christian marriage and maintains the value to the community of the Christian home, but it is not blind to the consequences of human frailty and sinfulness, and it recognises that there is a place for repentance. When the civil power has allowed the dissolution of a marriage, the Church, remembering that the purpose of God is ever redemptive, gives her blessing on a new marriage of either party to the former marriage, provided always that he or she has satisfied the Church's duly appointed representatives of a sincere repentance for any previous marriage fault, and of a desire to begin anew with the blessing of God and in true obedience to his will. The Minister and Congregation Committee are the appointed representatives of the Church. The Minister individually, and the Committee acting as a body, must be satisfied that the required conditions are present to permit a new marriage of divorced persons to be celebrated in the Church.'[33]

This chapter may fittingly conclude with illustrations of how differences in marriage discipline have been dealt with in actual schemes

32. *Minutes of Conference 1948*, p. 161.
33. Cf. the Resolution of the General Synod of the Moravian Church in the United States, 1957: 'That in every case where action is taken in regard to divorced persons, the Unitas Fratrum urges upon its pastors and congregations the need to make every effort to avoid both a rigid legalism and an irresponsible abuse in the discharge of their sacred responsibility.'

of church union, namely that which came to pass in 1947 in South India with the Anglican Church as one of the participants, and the projected unions in North India, Ceylon and Nigeria.

Chapter XII of the Constitution of the Church of South India deals with the Marriage Law of the Church. It recognises that differences of marriage discipline existed between the uniting Churches, and therefore the task of framing a marriage law can only be undertaken when the Churches have grown together and share one life: until then only provisional rules can be laid down. The Constitution declares that 'the Law of the Church relating to divorce must be governed by, and express, the fundamental principles and ideals of Christian marriage which were laid down by Christ and have throughout the centuries been followed by his Church'. As a consequence of this it is laid down that no Minister of the Church of South India 'may solemnise the marriage with any other person of either of two persons who have been married together as Christians (or having been married together as non-Christians have been received into the Church as husband and wife), so long as the other partner to the marriage is living; and any member of the Church who contracts such a marriage shall be liable to the discipline of the Church'. Nevertheless this rule is not in every case to be strictly enforced, for

> 'the Christian Church has always recognised that there are circumstances in which these ideals of Christian marriage cannot at once be attained, and that, especially in communities lately converted to Christianity, there are special cases in which the law of the Church should not be applied with rigidity, lest greater evils follow. In such cases therefore the Bishop of the Diocese, acting in accordance with such principles as may have been enunciated or such general directions as may have been laid down by the Synod of the Church, and after due investigation of all the circumstances of the individual case, shall have power to modify the strict letter of the law of the Church and to sanction the solemnisation of such marriages or to relax the discipline of the Church on those who contract such marriages'.[34]

The Constitution contains a clause safeguarding the right of a Minister to refuse to solemnise a marriage to which he has conscientious objections.

The Scheme of Church Union in North India and Pakistan contains

34. *Constitution of the Church of South India* (1956 edition), pp. 62-63.

a draft law of marriage in which Christ's 'principle and standard of marriage' is declared to be 'a lifelong and indissoluble union for better or for worse'. Its rulings on the matter of remarriage after divorce, and the provision it makes for exceptions in certain cases, follow closely those of the Church of South India.[35]

The Scheme of Church Union in Ceylon (Lanka) contains a recognition that 'with respect to the marriage-law of the Church there are differences of conviction both within and between the several uniting Churches'. According to Christ's teaching, marriage is a lifelong union and therefore the Church's rule must be not to solemnise a second marriage during a former partner's lifetime: nevertheless 'since there may be exceptional cases which warrant exceptional treatment, the Bishop in Court shall have power to dispense from the normal law of the Church of Lanka. Where such dispensation is made, no Minister shall be obliged to solemnise such a marriage contrary to his own convictions'. The Ceylon Scheme provides that when a divorced person is remarried civilly, the civil marriage may be followed by a Service of Prayer and Dedication, subject to the Bishop's approval and his directions for the holding of such a service. Provision is also made for a judgment of nullity. A person whose marriage has been dissolved and wishes to remarry may present his or her case to the Bishop in Court, who may decide that the case was one in which a decree of nullity could have been granted. So long as the grounds of nullity in civil law are consonant with the requirements of the Church, the Church of Lanka will recognise the nullity decrees of a civil court.[36]

The Constitution of the proposed United Church of Nigeria lays down that 'marriage is by divine institution an indissoluble, exclusive and lifelong partnership between one man and one woman'. No marriage can therefore be solemnised between Christians who have been previously married so long as the other partner in that marriage is still living. Nevertheless 'in special circumstances in which the law of the Church should not be applied with undue rigidity' the Bishop, after consultation with the Diocesan Standing Committee on Matters pertaining to Marriage, may sanction the solemnisation of a marriage which would otherwise be precluded, though no minister is obliged to solemnise a marriage against his conscience.[37]

35. *Plan of Church Union in North India and Pakistan* (Fourth edition, 1965), pp. 32-34.
36. *Scheme of Church Union in Ceylon* (Third edition 1955), pp. 62-63.
37. *The Constitution of the Church in Nigeria,* pp. 42-44.

It will be seen from the foregoing survey that the problem of divorce and remarriage is one that every Christian communion has had to face, with a view to laying down some form of marriage discipline for its ministers and members, or at least affording them guidance in making their own decisions. It will also be apparent that in the main this task has been carried out with wisdom, charity and a sense of deep responsibility, so that with the need to uphold, and bear witness to, Christ's standard of marriage is combined a compassionate understanding of human failure and the suffering which that failure causes in married life.

V

THE QUESTION OF NULLITY

It is impossible to consider the question of divorce without some reference to nullity, and indeed nullity has been mentioned more than once in the preceding pages. Divorce and nullity are to be clearly distinguished from each other. Divorce is the dissolution of an existing and valid marriage: nullity means that no marriage has existed. A decree of divorce is effective, in the sense that it dissolves (or at least purports to dissolve) a marriage: a decree of nullity is declaratory, stating a fact, namely, that an alleged marriage has never been a marriage. The grounds of divorce are factors arising subsequently to the marriage ceremony: the grounds of nullity must be factors present at the time of the marriage ceremony.[1]

Yet in spite of this distinction between divorce and nullity the two are often confused, and for this there is at least a measure of excuse. What is nullity has sometimes been called divorce, as for instance in Western Canon Law, which recognised no divorce in our modern sense of the word but allowed marriages to be declared null on a number of grounds. Hence the practice of referring to Henry VIII's 'divorce' of Katherine of Aragon, which was a case of nullity arising from a supposed impediment rendering Henry's marriage to Katherine invalid. The Canons of 1604 of the Church of England, as already mentioned, use the term 'divorce' to cover both the 'annulling of pretended matrimony' and divorce *a mensa et thoro,* or what is now called judical separation.

A further cause of confusion between divorce and nullity lies in the fact that marriages falling within the scope of nullity are of two kinds, void and voidable. A void marriage is one which in itself and from the outset is no marriage, and requires no judicial decision to make it so, though for the sake of certainty it may be wise to seek a decree. Want of age or an existing marriage, for example, render a marriage void. A voidable marriage is one that can be annulled on the petition of one of the parties, and when so annulled is declared null and void from the beginning: nevertheless it ranks as a valid marriage until it is judicially annulled.[2] Under the old ecclesiastical law impo-

1. K. E. Kirk, *Marriage and Divorce* (second edition), Chapter III; F. J. Sheed, *Nullity of Marriage,* (revised edition), pp. 7-8.
2. Sheed, op. cit., p. 25; A. T. Macmillan, *What is Christian Marriage?* pp. 110-111; *The Church and the Law of Nullity of Marriage,* pp. 19-20.

tence rendered a marriage voidable, but in England the category of voidable marriages has been enlarged by the additional grounds contained in the Matrimonial Causes Act of 1937. It may be noted that the doctrine of approbation obtains in English law in respect of voidable marriages: 'a party can so act in the way of approbating the marriage as to be precluded from subsequently disputing its validity'.[3] Thus it has been held that the adoption of a child 'approbates' a marriage so as to disallow a petition for nullity.[4]

The grounds of nullity are factors or circumstances which violate the conditions necessary for a valid marriage, and which therefore constitute 'impediments' to marriage. Certain impediments are common to both Canon and civil law.[5] An existing marriage is an impediment to marriage, save in so far as the law of the state may provide for the dissolution of a marriage. So are want of age, whatever be the minimum age which civil or ecclesiastical authority may fix for ability to consent to marriage,[6] and relationship within the prohibited degrees, however those degrees be defined.[7] Insanity, which excludes the possibility of consent, is an impediment to marriage, as is also force or fear used to extract consent, for forced consent is not true consent.

Roman Catholic Canon Law recognises further grounds of nullity, notably disparity of worship (*disparitas cultus*) and defective consent. A marriage between a baptised Christian and an unbaptised person or heathen is held to be void for disparity of worship, though it is subject to Papal dispensation. In the Church of England the marriage of a baptised to an unbaptised person is held to be valid though irregular, and bishops may require such cases to be referred to them. A factor of a special character would enter in if the non-Christian party were a Muslim or adherent of a religion which permitted polygamy, and therefore might not intend marriage in a Christian sense.

Defective consent is a ground of nullity in Roman Catholic Canon Law and results from the intention to exclude permanence or to ex-

3. *The Church and the Nullity of Marriage,* p. 20.
4. Slater v. Slater, 1953.
5. In addition to diriment impediments, which render a marriage void, Canon Law also recognises obstructive impediments, which render a marriage irregular though valid.
6. In English law since 1929 the age for both males and females is 16. The present Roman Catholic Canon Law fixes 16 for the man and 14 for the woman.
7. In England the revision of the Table of Kindred and Affinity in 1946 brought the ecclesiastical law into line with the civil law.

clude offspring. If the parties to a marriage enter into an agreement that the marriage shall be for a limited period, or that each party shall consent to a divorce if the other desires it, the marriage is void, because, permanence being excluded, the parties could not be said to consent to marriage but only to a temporary union or concubinage. The Marconi case, which came before the Roman Rota in 1927, was of this kind.[8] It should be noted that exclusion of permanence requires a positive act of will excluding indissolubility in respect of a particular marriage, and not merely a belief that marriage in general is not indissoluble.[9] An agreement to avoid the possibility of children by the practice of contraception would render a marriage null, on the ground that, by excluding the primary purpose of marriage, the parties would not have consented to marriage in the true sense.[10]

English civil law does not recognise defective consent as a ground of nullity. Any private reservation or agreement between the parties in limitation of consent would receive no countenance from the Courts, as being contrary both to public policy and to the nature of marriage as English law holds it to be.[11] Whether the Church of England should recognise defective consent as a ground of nullity and have machinery for examining possible cases will be discussed later.

The question of nullity has been prominently before the Church of England in recent years, and for two reasons: first, the additional grounds of nullity contained in the 1937 Act, and secondly, the widespread desire for some means by which certain civilly dissolved marriages could be declared null and the parties permitted to remarry with the rites of the Church. In 1949 the two Archbishops, at the request of the Convocations, appointed a Commission to examine the whole question of nullity, and its report, *The Church and the Law of Nullity of Marriage*, was published in 1955.

The 1937 Matrimonial Causes Act declared a marriage to be voidable if one of the parties at the time of the marriage was subject to recurrent fits of insanity or epilepsy or was suffering from a communicable venereal disease, or if the woman was pregnant by another man, and these facts were undisclosed to the other,party, who could petition for nullity within a year of the marriage taking place. These grounds would appear to have been accepted by the Church of England, and the Nullity Commission recommended that consideration

8. Sheed, *Nullity of Marriage*, pp. 33-34.
9. Ibid., pp. 34-36.
10. Ibid., pp. 42-45.
11. *The Church and the Law of Nullity of Marriage*, Chapter IV.

be given to their incorporation into Canon Law.[12] The implication is that if the true facts had been known, the other party would not have consented to the marriage. A precedent might be found in the now obsolete impediment of *error de qualitate,* or they could be justified on the more general ground that the contract to marry is *uberrimae fidei,* one in which there must be the utmost frankness between the parties. The principle here involved could obviously not be given indefinite extension, but mental disease, epilepsy, venereal disease and pregnancy by another man are factors affecting so seriously the matrimonial union that 'it would seem reasonable to see in these grounds a recognition by society of certain conditions which may be implicit in the marriage contract'.[13]

Of quite a different character is the other ground of nullity under the 1937 Act, namely, wilful refusal of consummation. It is difficult to see how the Church on its own principles, or the State for that matter, could accept this as a ground of nullity, seeing that it is an event subsequent to the marriage. Yet when this refusal is persisted in, it would seem only right that the other party should be able to secure release from the marriage. If release is granted by way of nullity, the justification must be that refusal of consummation is evidence of a psychological incapacity existing at the time of the marriage, and the Nullity Commission recommended this provision of the Act be repealed and be replaced by a provision that a Court may draw an inference of incapacity from the fact that consummation has been refused.[14] Alternatively, if release were by way of divorce, it could be held to be a special case and in no way a barrier to a second marriage with the blessing of the Church, and in favour of this appeal could be made to the principle of Canon Law, that though consent makes a marriage, consummation is necessary to its full indissolubility.

Complicated questions arise as to what precisely constitutes consummation. On this the civil courts have given different decisions, the authoritative judgment being that of the House of Lords in Baxter v. Baxter, 1948, according to which the use of contraceptives does not exclude consummation. The Roman Catholic Church adheres to the canonical requirement for consummation, namely the deposit of seed in the woman, which would rule out some, but not all, forms of intercourse with contraceptives. The Church of England Nullity Com-

12. Ibid., pp. 47-48.
13. Ibid., pp. 28-29.
14. Ibid., p. 48.

mission held that penetration is the only practical test of consummation.[15]

When divorce *a vinculo* with liberty of remarriage is not permitted, there is a very natural disposition to enlarge the scope of nullity, which was the case in the later Middle Ages, when the multiplication of impediments and the possibility of a technical flaw in a dispensation meant that grounds could nearly always be found for ending a marriage which there was a strong desire to end. It cannot be gainsaid that the renewed attention paid to nullity in recent years within Anglicanism has been largely the result of refusing remarriage in church after divorce, and this has led to the proposal that Church Courts should be established for the determination of applications for nullity. Two kinds of cases are envisaged as coming within the purview of the proposed Courts.

The first kind of case is that in which a marriage has been dissolved by divorce, but it is alleged that grounds existed on which a decree of nullity could have been sought. The comparative simplicity of divorce procedure compared with that of nullity, in which expert medical evidence is generally required, has undoubtedly led to divorce being sought in a number of cases in preference to nullity. It was with this situation in view that the Archbishops' Commission on Canon Law, which reported in 1947, included in draft Canon XXXVI, 'Of Holy Matrimony', a provision to the effect that if the Bishop of a diocese, sitting with his Chancellor, were satisfied that there were good grounds on which a marriage could have been annulled instead of being dissolved, he could allow either of the parties to be married in church, although the other party was still living.[16] Three influential members of the Commission, including Dr. Garbett, the Archbishop of York, dissented from this proposal, which was eventually dropped, and the whole question of nullity was referred, as previously mentioned, to a special Commission appointed by the Archbishops. The recommendation of the Commission was that, when a decree of divorce has been obtained and it is suggested that a decree of nullity might have been successfully sought, the Church should accept the decree of the Civil Court as final, but the help of the legal profession should be enlisted with a view to the avoidance of such cases.[17]

The other kind of case is that which falls under the heading of de-

15. Ibid., pp. 35 and 48.
16. *The Canon Law of the Church of England,* pp. 93 and 125-6.
17. *The Church and the Law of Nullity of Marriage,* pp. 44 and 48.

fective intention or defective consent. It has been argued, among others by the Bishop of Exeter, that not all marriages at the present time ought to be regarded as marriages in the Christian sense, in that the parties to them cannot necessarily be presumed to intend a life-long union. In the opinion of the Bishop

> 'both Church and State are insisting on regarding as valid marriages a number of unions which have never been marriages at all, because they were never intended to be such. The two parties, or perhaps only one of them, had every intention at the time of making the contract, of getting a divorce if the thing did not turn out well, or if either of them later met someone else with whom they would prefer to live. It was in this sense, and in this sense only, that they intended to "marry". They are therefore not married at all, and it ought to be possible to rebut the presumption that they are married more easily than is now the case'.[18]

Mr. A. T. Macmillan has similarly argued that the facilities which the State provides for divorce, and the prevailing public opinion concerning divorce, make it impossible any longer to assume that marriage as understood in this country is marriage in the Christian sense.[19] The Church, therefore, it is said, ought to have means, in the form of a court or tribunal, for giving an authoritative decision in such cases and to determine whether or not the previous dissolved marriage is a bar to a new marriage with the Church's blessing. Therein lies the significance of the qualification in the 1948 Lambeth Resolution disallowing the remarriage of divorced persons in church: 'unless it has been established that there exists no marriage bond recognised by the Church'.

In a number of Provinces of the Anglican Communion nullity procedures on these lines have been adopted. The 1946 Canon of the Protestant Episcopal Church of the United States, for example, are designed to bring under the head of nullity as many cases as possible of dissolved marriages. Among the impediments listed are 'such defects of personality as to make competent or free consent possible', by which presumably is meant a degree of psychological immaturity inconsistent with a full appreciation of the responsibilities of mar-

18. Lacey-Mortimer, *Marriage in Church and State,* p. 206.

19. Macmillan, *What is Christian Marriage?* pp. 141-3, and *Marriage, Divorce and the Church; Chaos or Reform - Which?,* pp. 9-12. The Rev. Walter Boulton adopts the same position, *Marriage* (second edition) pp. 70-72.

riage, and 'concurrent contract inconsistent with the contract establishing canonical marriage', which would cover any kind of private agreement for a trial marriage or a marriage terminable by mutual consent. Both of these are in effect instances of defective intention or consent. A similar procedure to that in the American Episcopal Church has been established under Part III of the 1967 Canon of the Anglican Church in Canada, and there are other Churches in the Anglican Communion in which the Bishop or a Diocesan Court may give a judgment of nullity.[20]

It is understandable that among the clergy of the Church of England there should have arisen a widespread demand for Church Courts or other machinery for investigating possible cases of nullity. The matter was considered by the Archbishops' Nullity Commission but their conclusion was unfavourable: 'The Commission does not, at any rate at the present time, recommend the establishment of Church Courts to deal with cases of alleged nullity, and considers that the use of any less formal machinery would be undesirable.'[21]

Disappointing as it may have been to some, the Commission's conclusion had weighty considerations to support it. So long as the Church of England is an established Church the Courts of the Church are also Courts of the Realm. To set up a new Church Court such as a Matrimonial or Nullity Court would require legislation, and it is highly doubtful whether the Crown's advisers or Parliament would agree to such legislation if the main purpose of the Court were to question or set aside judgments given in the civil matrimonial courts. If a Church Court were to handle cases of nullity, in which medical evidence might be decisive, there would have to be power to compel the attendance of witnesses, and Parliament would have to agree to the granting of this power, which it might well decline to do. It could not be exercised by any informal tribunal, or even by the Bishop sitting with his Chancellor.[22]

If defective intention were to be allowed by a Church Court as a ground of nullity, there would be the difficulty of deciding what constituted evidence, apart from the word of the parties, for such defective intention. Unless, as is hardly likely, private agreements or reservations made at the time of marriage were embodied in written documents, we should find ourselves entirely in the realm of the sub-

20. See ante, Chapter III.
21. *The Church and the Law of Nullity of Marriage,* p. 48.
22. Ibid., pp. 42-43.

jective, and it would be almost impossible to know what was in the minds of the parties perhaps many years previously, or what their intention was, if other than that expressed in the words by which they contracted marriage.

If the Church were to declare marriages null on a large scale because those who entered upon them could not be presumed to intend a lifelong union, it would tend to bring about a serious lowering of the general view of marriage. The Church might well solve certain problems of her own internal discipline, but at the cost of devaluing marriage in the eyes of the community as a whole. In spite of the facilities provided for divorce, marriage is still by the law of England 'the union of one man and one woman, voluntarily entered into for life, to the exclusion of all others',[23] and a statement to that effect is read before every Register Office marriage. The lifelong character of marriage is, of course still more explicitly expressed in the Prayer Book Marriage Service and in other forms of religious marriage. Moreover such a procedure as has been advocated would place a person who married thoughtlessly or carelessly, or who intended only a trial or temporary marriage, at an advantage compared with one whose marriage broke down in spite of his or her entering upon it with the highest and most serious intentions and in spite of every effort to make the marriage succeed.

Against whatever usefulness such Church Courts as have been proposed might possess must be set the dangers in which they might involve the Church. Here the warning of the late Bishop of Oxford, Dr. Kenneth Kirk, may be fittingly quoted:

> 'If a formal court begins to draw nice distinctions - to allow one couple to be married in church, whilst the privilege is denied to another - discontent will rapidly grow. Each pair of applicants will believe that their case is as much one for compassionate treatment as any other, and refusal even in a single instance will be broadcast far and wide as an example of a lack of that justice which ought to be administered by Courts Christian - a grief to the friends of the Church, a scandal to be pilloried by her critics and enemies . . . Rightly or wrongly the use of declarations of nullity by the Roman Church is widely suspect. It is not desirable that the Church of

23. This statement is based upon the words of Lord Penzance in Hyde v. Hyde and Woodmansee, 1866. In its original context the emphasis of the statement was upon 'to the exclusion of all others', as the marriage in question was a Mormon, and therefore potentially polygamous, one.

England should take a course which would inevitably attract similar suspicion to itself.'[24]

Granted its premises Roman Catholic practice in the matter of nullity probably works well and fairly.[25] The Roman Catholic Church has its corpus of Canon Law and its trained canonists; it has its Diocesan Courts and the Rota at Rome; and before a nullity is granted the *defensor vinculi* has to put the case against granting it. The Roman Catholic Church is - or has been up to the present, but great changes are now taking place - a predominantly juridical institution and its ethos authoritarian. The character of the Church of England is far removed from that of Rome, not least in that its approach to problems of discipline is pastoral rather than juridical. But nullity, if it is to be handled at all, can only be handled juridically, involving as it does highly complex issues of fact and law.[26] We may question whether it is either possible or desirable to reproduce the Roman system or anything like it in the very different circumstances of the Church of England.

24. *Marriage and Divorce* (second edition), pp. 131-2.
25. An explanation and defence of its working will be found in Sheed, *Nullity of Marriage,* and in the Catholic Truth Society pamphlet, *Nullity,* by Monsignor Hallett.
26. *The Church and the Law of Nullity of Marriage,* p. 42.

VI

THE ARCHBISHOP'S GROUP AND *PUTTING ASUNDER*

In 1951 Mrs Eirene White introduced a Bill in the House of Commons providing that when a husband and wife had lived apart for seven years, and there was no prospect of reconciliation, either of them might petition for divorce without having to prove a matrimonial offence by the other. After a second reading the Bill was withdrawn, the Government agreeing to appoint a Royal Commission to study the whole question of marriage and divorce. The Commission, which sat under the chairmanship of Lord Morton of Henryton, received evidence 'on behalf of the Church of England' from the Archbishop of Canterbury, Dr. Fisher, who vigorously opposed the suggestion that seven years' separation should be a ground of divorce. This, according to the Archbishop, rested upon no moral basis and destroyed the hitherto accepted principle of marriage; it was also capable of causing great social mischief by encouraging illicit relationships, those involved in them knowing that in time the relationship could always be regularised, and by inflicting insecurity and hardship upon innocent women.[1] The Royal Commission reported in 1955, nine of its members being in favour of making separation for a given period an additional ground of divorce,[2] nine being opposed to it, and one member, Lord Walker, urging the adoption of a new principle in place of that of the matrimonial offence, namely, irretrievable breakdown of marriage, defined as a situation in which 'the facts and circumstances affecting the lives of the parties adversely to one another are such as to make it improbable that an ordinary husband and wife would ever resume cohabitation'.[3]

In 1963 Mr Leo Abse introduced a Bill which revived the proposal in Mrs White's Bill of divorce after seven years' separation, but containing in addition provisions designed to promote reconciliation. To ensure the passage of these latter Mr Abse withdrew the other, and more controversial, part of his Bill. Strong opposition was voiced by

1. *The Church and Marriage* (1954), pp. 15-18. The Archbishop in his evidence recommended that 'wilful refusal of consummation' should be a ground of divorce or judicial separation and not of nullity, and he also opposed the proposal to legalise marriage with a divorced partner's sister or brother.
2. Of these nine, four members recommended that divorce should be allowed against the objections of one spouse, if in the opinion of the Court the separation was due at least in part to the conduct of the objecting spouse.
3. Royal Commission on Marriage and Divorce, 1951, *Report,* p. 340.

Church leaders to the proposal of divorce after seven years' separation, and a joint statement was issued in April 1963 by the Archbishops of Canterbury, York and Wales, the Roman Catholic Archbishop of Birmingham, and the Moderator and Secretary of the Free Church Federal Council. The statement condemned the proposal in question as likely to cause injustice to innocent parties in spite of the safeguards which the Bill contained, as introducing a new principle into the country's marriage laws and allowing in effect divorce by consent. Nevertheless in a significant final sentence the signatories declared themselves 'anxious to examine any measure for relieving hardships which would not sap the foundation of marriage'.[4] Later the Archbishop of Canterbury, Dr. Ramsey, speaking in the debate on the Bill in the House of Lords, said, 'If it were possible to find a principle at law of breakdown of marriage which was free from any trace of the idea of consent, which conserved the point that offences and not only wishes are the basis of breakdown, and which was protected by a far more thorough insistence on reconciliation procedure first, then I would wish to consider it'. The Archbishop added that he was asking some of his fellow-churchmen 'to see whether it is possible to work at this idea, sociologically as well as doctrinally, to discover if anything can be produced'.[5] The outcome was the appointment by the Archbishop in January 1964 of a group, consisting mainly but not entirely of members of the Church of England, to review the law of England concerning divorce and to consider whether there could be included in the law of the State a principle or procedure which would be likely to operate

> '(1) more justly and with greater assistance to the stability of marriage and the happiness of all concerned including children than at present;
>
> and (2) in such a way as to do nothing to undermine the approach of couples to marriage as a lifelong covenant.'[6]

The Church's discipline in the matter of divorce and remarriage did not fall within the Group's terms of reference, which were limited to a consideration of such changes in the law of the land as would promote the general welfare and at the same time not prejudice the stability of marriage.

4. *The Times,* 3rd April, 1963.
5. *Parliamentary Debates (Lords),* Vol. 250, cols. 1543-7.
6. *Putting Asunder,* p. ix.

In July, 1966, the Archbishop's Group reported in a document entitled *Putting Asunder: a Divorce Law for Contemporary Society,* which attracted widespread attention and also in many quarters admiration for the boldness of its proposals and the ability with which the case for them was argued.

The members of the Group were aware of the difficulty of the task they had undertaken. On the one hand there were those who would see in a body of Christians concerning themselves with the secular law of marriage only an example of ecclesiastical pressure, and on the other some Christians might fear that an attempt by the Church to improve the secular law would lead to a compromise of its witness to the teaching of Christ. The Group frankly recognised the existence of a plural society in which only a minority accepted the traditional Christian view of marriage, but at the same time it affirmed the Church's responsibility to the society in which it is set, a responsibility which in a special degree rests upon the Church of England by reason of its legal establishment and the part which historically it has played in the development of the matrimonial law. The Group expressed in the following terms its attitude to the task which it was commissioned to fulfil:

> 'It is right and proper for the Church to co-operate with the State, and for Christians to co-operate with secular humanists and others who are not Christians, in trying to make the divorce law as equitable and as little harmful to society as it can be made. Since *ex hypothesi* the State's matrimonial law is not meant to be a translation of the teaching of Jesus into legal terms, but allow properly for that "hardness of heart" of which Jesus himself took account, the standard by which it is to be judged is certainly not the Church's own canon law and pastoral discipline. Any advice that the Church tenders to the State must rest, not upon doctrines that only Christians accept, but upon premises that enjoy wide acknowledgement in the nation as a whole'.[7]

The recommendations of the Archbishop's Group were of a far-reaching character and called for a radical change in the existing law of divorce. This law (with one exception) is based upon the concept of the matrimonial offence, that is, a wrong done by one party to the other by adultery, desertion or cruelty, and entitling the injured party to redress in the form of release from the marriage. (The excep-

7. *Putting Asunder,* p. 12.

tion is, of course, incurable insanity, which is a misfortune and not an offence.) The Group recommended the total abandonment of the principle of the matrimonial offence as a ground of divorce, and the substitution for it of a new and comprehensive ground, namely, the breakdown of marriage. The only place which would be left for the matrimonial offence would be as evidence tending to support the breakdown of marriage.

The Group enumerated a number of objections to the doctrine of the matrimonial offence. It 'commits the courts to a superficial conception of the relationship between husband and wife'. The matrimonial offence is as often as not the symptom rather than the cause of the marriage failure. Then, too, the present law entails an accusatorial procedure which is remote from realities: 'if the parties are agreed that there is no solution to their problem except divorce, they must not tell the court so; they must pretend that the wrongdoing of one is such that the other is forced to apply for relief'.[8] An intolerable situation can be ended only if a suitable offence is afforded by the history of the marriage, or if, in the event of those concerned not being too scrupulous, one can be contrived. Spouses may commit offences, or purport to do so, in order to end the situation. In effect, according to the Group, the present law admits divorce by consent. Again, the terms 'innocent' and 'guilty' in this context often bear little relation to reality. The party who is guilty of the matrimonial offence may not be the party bearing the greater responsibility for the breakdown of the marriage, and there are frequent cases in which a petitioner has to ask for the court's discretion in respect of his or her own misconduct. Finally the present law itself breaks with the doctrine of the matrimonial offence in making insanity a ground of divorce.[9]

In place of the present accusatorial procedure the Group suggested a procedure by inquest, that is to say, an enquiry into the past history and the present state of a marriage, with a view to ascertaining whether anything remains of a genuine personal relationship between the parties or what the prospects are of the broken relationship being repaired. The Group quoted with qualified approval the words of Lord Walker concerning marriage breakdown in the *Report* of the 1951 Royal Commission:

'The true significance of marriage as I see it is lifelong cohabita-

8. Ibid., p. 29.

9. Ibid., p. 30-31.

tion in the home for the family. But when the prospect of continuing cohabitation has ceased, the true view as to the significance of marriage seems to require that the legal tie should be dissolved. Each empty tie - as empty ties accumulate - adds increasing harm to the community and injury to the ideal of marriage.'[10]

In such an enquiry or inquest there would be no 'innocent' or 'guilty' party and no victory of one spouse over the other, but a divorce would be seen to be what in fact it is, 'a defeat for both, a failure of the marital "two-in-oneship" in which both its members, however unequal their responsibility, are inevitably involved together'.[11] Among the factors to be considered in an inquest on a marriage would be actions which are at present grounds of divorce (though they would be no longer in themselves grounds of divorce), the length of time the parties had been living separately from each other, and the outcome of any efforts that had been made at reconciliation.

In the opinion of the Group the doctrine of breakdown is in line with certain tendencies discernible in the way the existing law is now administered. There is the wide exercise of the court's discretion in cases of a petitioner's misconduct, which in effect often means an enquiry into, and a judgment upon, the total matrimonial situation. Again the highest judicial authority has ruled that cruelty as a ground of divorce need not be malicious or intentional, but can be any conduct leading to a situation which the petitioner ought not to have to endure.[12] 'In practice, then,' says *Putting Asunder,* 'the law is moving away from basing divorce on a finding concerning the delinquency of one of the parties towards basing it on a finding concerning the state of the marriage relationship and the demands of distributive justice'.[13]

A point on which the Archbishop's Group lay great emphasis is that breakdown of marriage must be the sole ground of divorce and not merely an addition to the existing grounds. This is where the recommendations of the Group differ from the provisions in Mrs White's and Mr Abse's Bills and from the law in force in Australia and New Zealand.[14] The two principles of breakdown and matrimonial

10. *Report,* p. 341, quoted in *Putting Asunder,* p. 37. Of the view expressed by Lord Walker the Group says, 'This view of the matter is not that which is taken by Christians as such. But it seems to us not an unworthy or improper conception for the law of a secular society to uphold.'
11. *Putting Asunder,* p. 18.
12. Gollins v. Gollins, and Williams v. Williams, House of Lords, 1963.
13. *Putting Asunder,* p. 37.
14. Recent divorce legislation in New Zealand and Australia is described in *Putting Asunder,* pp. 100-111.

offence are basically incompatible, as are the attitudes and procedures which they demand. Were the two principles to co-exist there would be, the Group considered, a tendency to grant decrees whenever the existence of an offence could be proved without any genuine trial of the issue of breakdown. To make breakdown an additional, and not the exclusive, ground would be to 'make divorce easier to get without really improving the law'. Breakdown would be pleaded 'as a last resort by petitioners who found they could not succeed on any other ground'. Failing the replacement of matrimonial offence by breakdown, the Group considered that it would be preferable to retain the existing law and to concentrate on improving its administration.[15]

Among the objections to the doctrine of breakdown considered by the Group were the following: 'that the doctrine of breakdown entails "divorce by consent" ' and 'that it would be gravely unjust to permit divorce against the will of an unoffending spouse'. The Group replied to the first objection by pointing out that it would not be the parties themselves but the court that would decide whether the marriage should be dissolved. The issue of breakdown would have to be tried, and if the court were not satisfied that the marriage had irrevocably broken down, a decree would be refused in spite of the agreement of the parties. Equally 'the agreement of the parties in wanting a divorce would not be a bar, and might even count in favour of a divorce', though not in itself sufficing to effect a divorce.[16] In answer to the second objection the Group distinguished three factors which were involved, namely, the unoffending party's economic deprivation, the loss of matrimonial status, and the possibility that a petitioner might benefit by his or her own wrong. Economic deprivation could at least in part be avoided by the court's requiring as the condition of a decree a satisfactory arrangement concerning property, pensions and maintenance,[17] and in the opinion of the Group the behaviour of the spouses during the marriage could rightly be taken into account when assessing maintenance.[18]

Loss of matrimonial status is a matter of a different order for which no compensation is possible. 'Divorce', in the words of the Group, 'is the unnatural tearing asunder of what was meant to be indivisible, and the pain of it is bound to affect a faithful spouse more bitterly

15. *Putting Asunder*, pp. 59-60.
16. Ibid., p. 41.
17. Ibid., p. 48.
18. Ibid., p. 72.

than an unfaithful'.[19] The charge of injustice might be unanswerable if the divorce-situation were seen in terms of 'innocent' and 'guilty' parties, but if the issue being tried were whether or not the marriage-relationship were dead, there would be no question of a decree being granted in favour of one partner or against the other. The decree would do no more than record a fact.[20] A similar answer could be made to the objection based on the maxim that none should benefit by his own wrong. If the principle of breakdown were accepted, a decree of divorce would be seen 'not as a right gained by one suitor at the cost of the other, but as a judicial recognition of a state of affairs with consequent redefinition of status'.[21] Nevertheless no decree should be granted against the wish of an unoffending spouse if to grant it would be against the public interest and 'shake confidence in the administration of justice and cast doubt on the reality of the State's concern for marriage'.[22]

The Archbishop's Group showed itself fully aware of the changes which the substitution of breakdown for matrimonial offence would involve in the constitution and procedure of the courts, and these were dealt with in an appendix by a legally qualified member of the Group, Mr Quentin Edwards. One of the main concerns of the court under the new procedure would be to ensure that every attempt at reconciliation had been made. If not satisfied that the possibilities of reconciliation had been exhausted, the court should have power to adjourn the hearing.[23] One of the Group's recommendations was the appointment of 'forensic social workers', who could 'verify attempts at reconciliation, test the reliability of assertions made to the court and investigate any other matters on which the court wishes to be informed, and could report on the circumstances of children of the family'.[24]

The report of the Archbishop's Group, *Putting Asunder,* was referred by the Lord Chancellor, Lord Gardiner, to the Law Commission, a body set up under the Law Commissions Act of 1965 for the purpose of promoting the reform of the law. In November, 1966, there was presented to Parliament the Law Commission's report, entitled *Reform of the Grounds of Divorce: the Field of Choice,* in which appreciative but critical consideration was given to the proposals contained in *Putting Asunder.*

19. Ibid., p. 49.
20. Ibid., p. 50.
21. Ibid., p. 52.
22. Ibid., p. 53.
23. Ibid., p. 64.
24. Ibid., p. 70.

The Law Commissioners defined the objectives of a good divorce law as follows:

'(1) To buttress, rather than to undermine, the stability of marriage; and

(2) When, regrettably, a marriage has irretrievably broken down, to enable the empty legal shell to be destroyed with the maximum fairness and the minimum bitterness, distress and humiliation.'[25]

These objectives, in the view of the Commissioners, were not being adequately achieved by the present divorce law based on the principle of the matrimonial offence, upon which they passed this severe adverse judgment:

'It does not do all it might to aid the stability of marriage, but tends rather to discourage attempts at reconciliation. It does not enable all dead marriages to be buried, and those that it buries are not always interred with the minimum of distress and humiliation. It does not achieve the maximum possible fairness to all concerned, for a spouse may be branded as guilty in law though not the more blameworthy in fact. The insistence on guilt and innocence tends to embitter relationships, with particularly damaging results to the children, rather than to promote future harmony.'[26]

Convinced of the need for changes in the divorce law the Commissioners considered the various proposals put forward for reform, under the following headings: breakdown with inquest, breakdown without inquest, divorce by consent, and separation-ground. In their consideration of the proposals the main emphasis was laid upon their practicability or otherwise in the light of contemporary social facts and public opinion.

The procedure represented by the term 'breakdown with inquest' was that advocated by the Archbishop's Group, whose proposals were viewed with sympathy by the Commissioners for 'their rejection of exclusive reliance on matrimonial offence' but were nevertheless rejected as 'procedurally impracticable'.[27] They doubted the desirability of an inquest on the marriage in all cases, for the distress and humiliation it would cause would be inconsistent with the second requirement of a good divorce law. 'Public opinion', they said, 'would

25. *Reform of the Grounds of Divorce: the Field of Choice*, p. 10.
26. Ibid., p. 16.
27. Ibid., p. 54.

be unlikely to regard it as an improvement if in every case the whole matrimonial history were ventilated in public', and 'if our divorce laws are to be made more humane, it seems to us that the undefended divorce affords a better model than the dilatory, expensive and distressing defended divorce'.[28] The reconstitution of the courts would have to be more radical than the Archbishop's Group seemed to contemplate. The time and the cost of proceedings would be greatly increased, and it is doubtful if trained social workers such as the Group envisaged could be found in sufficient numbers. The Commissioners endorsed the emphasis placed by the Group on reconciliation, but there was a danger that the proposals as they stood might encourage parties to treat reconciliation procedures as a mere pre-petition formality.[29]

Rejecting as impracticable 'breakdown with inquest', the Commissioners went on to consider the alternatives. If the principle of 'breakdown without inquest' were adopted it would mean that the fact of the parties' separation and the resort to divorce proceedings could be taken as an indication that the marriage had broken down. The period of separation suggested by the Commissioners, if breakdown were to be the sole ground, was six months prior to the filing of the petition.[30] Consent would be practicable only as an additional and not the exclusive ground of divorce, and would be acceptable only where there were no dependent children. Even in the case of childless marriages it might lead to the dissolution of marriages which had not irretrievably broken down.[31] What the Commissioners termed 'separation-ground' denoted a period of separation as a ground of divorce additional to the existing grounds based on the matrimonial offence. In this case the Commissioners recommended that two periods of separation should be laid down, a shorter period (say, two years) after which a petitioner could secure a divorce in the absence of objection from the other partner, and a longer period (say, five or seven years) after which a petitioner could secure a divorce even if the other partner objected.[32] The Commissioners regarded all three alternative proposals as practicable in the sense that they could be implemented without serious legal difficulty and would not be contrary to public opinion,[33] but they did not go further in the direction of making more specific recommendations.

28. Ibid., p. 32.
29. Ibid., p. 33.
30. Ibid., pp. 36-39.
31. Ibid., pp. 39-42.
32. Ibid., pp. 44-47.
33. Ibid., p. 54.

Both the Archbishop's Group and the Law Commissioners were agreed that the restriction on petitions for divorce within three years of marriage should be retained.[34]

The subject of Divorce Law Reform was discussed in the House of Lords at the end of November, 1966, and the debate largely centred upon the proposals in *Putting Asunder* and the Law Commission's Report. The Archbishop of Canterbury and the Bishop of Exeter both attacked the proposal of divorce by consent, to which the Law Commissioners had given a limited approval, and defended the main principle underlying the proposals in *Putting Asunder,* namely, that breakdown of marriage should constitute the sole ground of divorce.[35] The Bishop of Exeter made the suggestion that a delay between divorce and the possibility of a second marriage was highly desirable. 'In my experience', he said, 'of dealing with marriages after divorce - and I have had to deal with a good many - those which have proved most stable were almost invariably those contracted some time after the divorce and having nothing to do with the obtaining of the divorce'.[36] Strong criticism of *Putting Asunder* came from Baroness Summerskill, who called it 'a curious and disappointing document', whose proposals 'will baffle the churchgoer' and whose recommendations 'are calculated to astonish a scientific humanist'. In her opinion its proposals failed to do justice to the need for family stability and the woman's need for security, and could only be interpreted as 'a rejection of the lifelong marriage contract and the substitution of trial marriage'.[37] In his speech in the Lords the Archbishop of Canterbury expressed the hope that the members of his Group might enter into discussions with members of the Law Commission with a view to seeing if the differences between them could be bridged, but he added the proviso that 'breakdown must not merely be made identical with separation as such, and breakdown must not be made identical with consent as such'.[38]

Endorsement of the proposals in *Putting Asunder* came from the Church Assembly in February, 1967, when a motion on divorce law reform proposed by Mr R. C. W. Gooch, a solicitor member of the Assembly, combined with an amendment moved by Professor J. N. D.

34. *Putting Asunder,* p. 64; *Reform of the Grounds of Divorce,* pp. 53 and 55.
35. *Parliamentary Debates (Lords),* Vol. 278, Cols. 243-6 and 273-8.
36. Ibid., Col. 247.
37. Ibid., Col. 291.
38. Ibid., Cols. 273-4.

Anderson, was passed by a large majority. The amended motion was passed in the following terms:

'That this Assembly

(1) affirms the Church's belief in the Christian principle of marriage as a lifelong partnership of one man and one woman;

(2) recognising the unsatisfactory state of the present law of divorce, views sympathetically any attempts to alter and improve it which would have the effect of increasing the stability of marriage;

(3) welcomes the report of the Group appointed by the Archbishop of Canterbury entitled *Putting Asunder,* and believes that the fact that a marriage appears finally to have broken down should be the sole ground of civil divorce;

(4) emphasises the Church's compassionate concern for all those who have been divorced or who suffer in any way from the operation of the laws of marriage and divorce;

(5) requests their Graces the Archbishops to instruct the Convocations of Canterbury and York to consider ways in which the Church can better exercise its pastoral ministry towards all such people, including those of them who remarry.'[39]

On 5th May, 1967, an important speech was made by the Lord Chancellor to the annual conference of the National Marriage Guidance Council at Brighton, and in this speech he indicated how in his opinion the principle of breakdown could be adopted without abandoning entirely the concept of the matrimonial offence. Breakdown of marriage should be the sole ground of divorce, but a matrimonial offence could still be taken into account without making it the basis of relief. 'Adultery, desertion, or intolerable conduct towards one's spouse', said Lord Gardiner, 'are often very reliable indications that the marriage has in fact broken down. I would have thought that such offences could properly be used by the law as guide posts pointing, in the absence of evidence to the contrary, or forgiveness, to breakdown'.[40] Here the Lord Chancellor was stating in other words what had been said in *Putting Asunder.*[41] It is significant that following this speech the Lord Chancellor was attacked by Mr Abse as going against

39. Church Assembly, *Report of Proceedings,* Spring Session 1967, pp. 231-267.
40. *The Times,* 6th May, 1967.
41. *Putting Asunder,* p. 18.

the report of his Law Commissioners and capitulating to the views of the Church.[42]

Further endorsement of the proposals in *Putting Asunder* was received in June, 1967, from the Christian Citizenship Department of the Methodist Church, whose report, approved by the Methodist Conference, recommended that breakdown of marriage should be the one comprehensive ground of divorce and that matrimonial offences should be taken as 'strong indications', but not proofs, of breakdown. In the absence of rebuttal the following should be taken as indications of breakdown:

'(a) Adultery which the petitioner finds impossible to forgive;
(b) Conduct by the respondent of a kind as intolerable that it would be unreasonable to expect the petitioner to continue to cohabit;
(c) A period of separation of two years, when the respondent with full knowledge of the consequences does not object, or the respondent has deserted;
(d) A period of separation of five years when the respondent objects'.[43]

In the Lords' debate the Archbishop of Canterbury had expressed the hope that the Law Commissioners and the Group responsible for *Putting Asunder* would enter into discussions with a view to seeing if the differences between them could be bridged. These discussions resulted in the publication by the Law Commission in August 1967 of a document embodying a consensus of opinion between the two bodies,[44] which the Law Commissioners believed to represent a workable law, and the Archbishop's Group considered to contain the essentials of *Putting Asunder.*[45]

The main proposals contained in the 'Consensus' were the following: divorce should be available only upon proof of irretrievable breakdown; a petitioner's solicitor should be required to certify to the court whether he had discussed with the petitioner the possibility of reconciliation and given information concerning those able to help in reconciliation; the court should have power to order an adjournment of up to three months so that the possibility of reconciliation

42. *The Times,* 6th May, 1967.
43. Methodist Christian Citizenship Department, memorandum *Reform of the Law on Divorce.*
44. The document was printed in *The New Law Journal* of 3rd August, 1967.
45. Article by Murray Sayle in *The Sunday Times,* 12th November, 1967.

could be explored; and on the question of evidence of breakdown the Commission proposed that

> 'No marriage shall be treated as having broken down irretrievably unless the court was satisfied that:
> (a) the respondent had committed adultery and the petitioner found it intolerable to continue or resume cohabitation; or
> (b) the conduct of the respondent had been so intolerable that the petitioner could not reasonably be expected to continue or resume cohabitation; or
> (c) the parties had ceased to cohabit for a continuous period of at least two years and the respondent either
> (i) had deserted the petitioner, or (ii) did not object to the grant of a divorce; or
> (d) the parties had ceased to cohabit for a continuous period of not less than five years.'

The proposals of the Law Commission as outlined in the 'Consensus' were embodied in a private member's Bill introduced into the House of Commons by Mr William Wilson, which received its second reading on 9th February, 1968, by a majority of 159 votes to 63. The Bill makes breakdown of marriage the sole ground of divorce, and evidence of breakdown is to be afforded by one or more of the facts listed in Section 2 (1) of the Bill:

> '(a) that since the celebration of the marriage the respondent has committed adultery and the petitioner finds it intolerable to live with the respondent;
> (b) that since the celebration of the marriage the respondent has behaved in such a way that the petitioner cannot reasonably be expected to live with the respondent;
> (c) that the respondent has deserted the petitioner without cause for a continuous period of at least two years immediately preceding the presentation of the petition;
> (d) that the parties to the marriage have lived apart for a continuous period of at least two years immediately preceding the presentation of the petition and the respondent does not object to a decree being granted;
> (e) that the parties to the marriage have lived apart for a continuous period of at least five years immediately preceding the presentation of the petition'.

If one or more of these facts is proved the court shall grant a decree 'unless it is satisfied on all the evidence that the marriage has not broken down irretrievably'. Provisions designed to encourage reconciliation form part of the Bill, and the court is given power to refuse a decree if the petitioner has attempted to deceive the court, or if satisfactory financial provision is not made for either party or for the children of the marriage. It will be noted that neither cruelty nor incurable insanity, which are grounds under the 1937 Act, appear here among the grounds for inferring breakdown, as presumably they are held to be sufficiently covered by the provisions concerning intolerable conduct and living apart.

The Divorce Reform Bill represents an attempt to embody in practice the main recommendations contained in *Putting Asunder,* but when judged in the light of the latter it appears very much a compromise, and indeed it was so described by the Archbishop of Canterbury.[46] The main difference between the Bill and *Putting Asunder,* of which it was in part the outcome, is this: that the 'breakdown with inquest' of *Putting Asunder* has become in the Bill 'breakdown without inquest', or at least without an inquest as thorough and as detailed as that envisaged by the authors of *Putting Asunder.*[47]

Following the second reading of the Bill, an article by the Archbishop of Canterbury appeared in a Sunday newspaper[48] in which he expressed serious reservations concerning the wisdom of some of its provisions. The Bill in his opinion extends the grounds of divorce by allowing breakdown of marriage to be inferred on grounds wider than those of the present divorce law: it retains in effect the matrimonial offence and adds two new grounds. The two-year separation clause will be an encouragement to couples who agree to enter upon a temporary marriage, and the five-year clause will be the cause of great hardship to many innocent spouses[49] and 'make intervention in a

46. The Archbishop speaking to students at Manchester University on 19th January said, 'The Bill that appeared this week is a kind of compromise. As usually happens in a compromise it contains bits that are very good and bits that are very bad.' *The Times,* 20th January, 1968.

47. The procedure proposed by the Archbishop's Group will be found in Chapter 6 and Appendix C of *Putting Asunder.* It was this procedure that the Law Commission considered impracticable and in some respects undesirable.

48. 'My Doubts about the Divorce Bill', *The Sunday Times,* 11th February, 1968. A reply to the Archbishop by Professor J. N. D. Anderson, a member of the Archbishop's Group, appeared in the following week's issue.

49. But the Archbishop's Group admitted that their proposals would permit a divorce against the wish of an unoffending spouse, and though realising the need to minimise the suffering involved, they were obliged to say that 'when a marriage comes to grief wounding cannot be avoided'. *Putting Asunder,* p. 49.

marriage more attractive to an adventurer or adventuress' by holding out the prospect of regularising the situation in five years' time. While the Archbishop welcomed parts of the Bill, such as the encouragement of reconciliation and the attempt to safeguard the interests of the faithful partner and of the children, he doubted 'whether this Bill will maintain the stability of marriage as its sponsors claim. It would seem that it could create more injustice and unhappiness than it could remove'.

It remains to be seen how far the Archbishop's view of the Bill will be endorsed by church opinion generally, but his criticisms will undoubtedly command a considerable measure of agreement, and not exclusively among church people.[50]

50. The Bill was welcomed by the Bishop of Durham, and in more qualified terms by the Bishops of Exeter and Leicester. *Church Times,* 19th January, 1968. It was strongly opposed in a statement by the Mothers' Union Marriage Group, *Church Times,* 9th February, 1968. The Bill was severely criticised by a leading divorce lawyer, Mr Geoffrey Crispin, Q.C., in *The Times,* 27th January, 1968. Baroness Summerskill, a leading feminist, has vigorously opposed the Bill on the ground of what she considers its injustice to women.

VII

A MARRIAGE DISCIPLINE FOR THE FUTURE

For the past thirty years practice in the Church of England regarding remarriage after divorce has been that recommended by successive Lambeth Conferences and laid down in the resolutions of the Convocations, those of the Canterbury Convocation being declared an Act of Convocation in 1957. These resolutions lay down that no marriage after divorce during the other partner's lifetime may be solemnised in church, but that those who have remarried after divorce may be admitted to Holy Communion on the recommendation of the incumbent and at the discretion of the Bishop. There is much that can be said in support of the marriage discipline embodied in the Convocation decisions. It has received the loyal adherence of the overwhelming majority of the clergy, and has made possible uniformity of practice throughout the Church of England in spite of differences of conviction concerning indissolubility. It has sought to combine a steadfast witness to the Christian standard of marriage as a lifelong union with a concern for the spiritual good of those who have fallen short of that standard. The refusal of remarriage in church has come to be generally understood and accepted, so that, to judge from the experience of many of the parish clergy, few requests are now received for the marriage of divorced persons in church, compared with the number of requests twenty or so years ago. With regard to the admission of remarried divorced persons to Communion, it would be generally acknowledged that the bishops have exercised their pastoral responsibility in the matter with sympathy and with a genuine desire to make available to all who feel their need of them the fellowship of the Church and the grace of the sacraments. What cannot of course be known is how many have turned regretfully away from the Church for what has seemed to them a harsh and unyielding attitude towards those who have experienced the bitterness of disappointed hopes in marriage.

Yet with all that can be said in defence of the present marriage discipline of the Church of England there are factors which give rise to serious questionings and misgivings.

There is first the question whether the present procedure is founded on any basis of principle or logic. In the past the attempt has seldom been made to defend it logically, and refuge has been taken in the dictum that 'life is greater than logic'. But it is doubtful whether, after all, the claims of consistency can be so easily dismissed. There can be only one reason for refusing to solemnise a marriage after divorce in church, and that is, that it is not a marriage as Christians understand marriage. But experience shows that second marriages after divorce are followed in many cases by the establishment of truly Christian homes and by a united and happy Christian family life: often, to quote Archbishop Fisher, 'a second marriage has by every test of the Holy Spirit that we are able to recognise been abundantly blessed'. Are we to say that these second marriages cannot be marriages at all in the Christian sense and therefore not qualified to receive the blessing of the Church, even though they are subsequently by implication recognised when the parties are admitted to Communion? Michael Keeling has recently pointed out what he calls the 'theological double-think' in the present position, and has written: 'The only logical conclusion from the established pastoral practice of admitting people to Communion who have been divorced and remarried is that remarriage after divorce is a permissible state. Faced with real pastoral needs the Church of England has recognised in practice what it is not yet ready to recognise in theory.'[1]

A second factor which makes some at least of the clergy unhappy about the present situation is its lack of constitutional authority. As has been pointed out, a resolution, and for that matter an Act, of Convocation has the authority only of a strong expression of corporate opinion or at most a recommendation, and not the binding force of a Canon. It may well have been the case that the resolution of Convocation dealing with the marriage of divorced persons had considerable spiritual authority when first passed, but can it be said still to possess that authority when it was deliberately determined not to seek its enactment as a Canon, and that because it would rob the clergy of a liberty which some of them conscientiously valued and because of the opposition which the proposed Canon would encounter in Parliament on the ground that it abolished this liberty? In view of the importance attached to Canon Law revision and of the officially expressed need for a generally accepted body of Canons drawn up in the light of modern conditions, it is hard to see how authority could any longer be claimed for a resolution, concerning a matter both of theological principle and also of deep practical concern to church people, after it was decided not to embody it in a Canon solely be-

1. Keeling, *Morals in a Free Society*, p. 94.

cause of the likelihood of objection by Parliament and failure to secure the Royal Assent. Either of two courses would have been preferable to the ambiguous one which was in fact adopted: on the one hand the Church could have gone ahead and faced the consequences in the knowledge that it was taking its stand on a principle, or on the other it could have decided that being a matter on which (in the Archbishop's words) 'it would be unwise to seek battle with Parliament' the remarriage of divorced persons was one which could be left to the responsible discretion of the clergy, as it was left by the State under the 1937 Act.[2]

A further reason for disquiet is the automatic exclusion of remarried divorced persons from Holy Communion, pending the submission of their case to the bishop and their readmission by him. Here is the virtual, indeed the actual, excommunication of a whole group of persons otherwise qualified to receive the sacrament of our Lord's appointment. Opinions may differ as to whether it is right or fitting to use the Holy Communion, the sacrament which proclaims Christ's universal redemption, as a means of registering disapproval or maintaining discipline, but so serious a matter as exclusion from Holy Communion is one that would require to have behind it the full sanction of law. But the law as to exclusion from Holy Communion is plain. It is embodied in the rubric of the Prayer Book which authorises only those to be excluded who are 'open and notorious evil livers' or persons between whom there is irreconcilable hatred and malice, and no resolution of Convocation can lawfully avail to enlarge the category of excluded persons. Those who have remarried after divorce, however much the Church may disapprove their action, cannot be regarded as 'open and notorious evil livers'. At a time when the Church disapproved of marriage to a deceased wife's sister Archbishop Randall Davidson wrote of exclusion from Communion in such a case: 'If justification were to be pleaded for such refusal of Holy Communion it must presumably be based upon the Rubric which allor enjoins the exclusion of "an open and notorious evil liver". It is in my judgment impossible rightly to apply these words on account of their marriage to a man and wife who have contracted as a civil contract a marriage expressly sanctioned by English law'.[3] He referred to the exclusion from Communion as 'the gravest censure which we can

2. On this the brief but pregnant article by P. R. P. Barker, 'Visible Justice', *Theology*, February 1964, deserves to be read.
3. G. K. A. Bell, *Randall Davidson*, p. 554.

legally lay upon an evil-doer', and we may ask whether those who have remarried after divorce are all to be held deserving of such a censure, even though it be a temporary one capable of being lifted at the bishop's discretion.

The feeling is undoubtedly growing in the Church of England that the time has come for a re-examination of the whole question of re-marriage in church after divorce. At the February 1967 session of the Church Assembly, following the debate on *Putting Asunder,* a motion on the subject was proposed in the following terms by Canon D. K. Dean and carried: 'That this Assembly requests the Convocations to give fresh consideration to the question of the marriage in church of persons who have been divorced.'[4] In the following October the question was brought before the Convocation of Canterbury by the Bishop of Worcester who proposed the setting up of a committee, empowered to confer with any similar committee set up by the Convocation of York, 'to consider ways in which the Church can better exercise its pastoral ministry towards all those who have been divorced, including those who remarry; and give fresh consideration to the question of marriage in church of persons who have been divorced'.[5] The Upper House, however, felt doubts about the wisdom of setting up such a committee, and resolved 'that this House, believing that the Christian theology of marriage must be the foundation of the Church's marriage discipline and ministry towards divorced persons, and taking account also of conversations with other Churches and possible changes in the civil law, does not favour at present the setting up of a Committee in the terms of the Bishop of Worcester's motion'.[6] A motion proposed by Canon Paul Welsby was carried in Full Synod requesting the Archbishop of Canterbury, in consultation with the Archbishop of York, 'to appoint a group of theologians to present a statement on the Christian doctrine of marriage'.[7]

The need for a reconsideration of the Church's attitude to divorce and remarriage has been given added urgency by the publication of *Putting Asunder* and the welcome accorded to that document by the Church Assembly. It is true that the Archbishop's Group saw its role solely as one of considering what changes in the secular law of divorce

4. Church Assembly, *Report of Proceedings,* Spring Session 1967, pp. 267-271.
5. *Chronicle of Convocation,* October 1967, pp. 242.
6. Ibid., p. 266.
7. Ibid., p. 276. The Group was appointed in March 1968, with Professor Howard Root as Chairman.

might be in the interests of the community, and expressly disclaimed any concern with the Church's discipline in the matter of divorce;[8] nevertheless it is doubtful whether such a dichotomy can ultimately be sustained, and the line of reasoning adopted in *Putting Asunder* must surely in the end exercise an influence upon the way in which the Church approaches the question of divorce and remarriage in respect of its internal discipline. The Church cannot in one context assert the principle of irretrievable breakdown, namely, that when all personal reality has gone out of a marriage, the marriage may be regarded as at an end, and in another context maintain that though all personal relationship has ceased to exist between the parties, they are still bound together by the *vinculum* or tie of marriage.

We enter here into the realm of ultimate theological convictions. Christian theology is committed to the affirmation that God is personal, and that in himself, as the doctrine of the Trinity implies, there is a fullness of personal relationships. As made in God's image human beings are persons, and God stands to them, and they to him, in a personal relationship. This truth, which is central to the whole New Testament revelation, has often in the course of Christian history been obscured, whether by legalism or by a quasi-magical sacramentalism. There is profound insight in the saying of James Denney that what the Reformation 'did in principle was to expel *things* from religion and to exhibit all its realities as persons and the relations of persons'.[9] It was for this reason that Erasmus contrasted with the later mediaeval legalistic view of marriage the humane view which sees the essence of marriage in mutual love, respect and companionship.[10] It was for this reason that later Bishop Hall and Bishop Cosin held that the reality of marriage consisted in the sharing of bed and board, and that the notion of a *vinculum* apart from this was 'merely chimerical and fancy'.[11]

Nothing that has so far been said must be taken as calling into question the permanence of marriage in God's intention, or as ignoring the place of forgiveness in the marriage relationship. It is God's will that marriage should be lifelong and the personal relationship in mar-

8. 'How the doctrine of Christ concerning marriage should be interpreted and applied within the Christian Church is one question: what the Church ought to say and do about secular laws of marriage and divorce is another question altogether. This can hardly be repeated too often.' *Putting Asunder,* pp. 3 and 4.
9. *The Christian Doctrine of Reconciliation,* p. 91.
10. In *Institutio Christiani Matrimonii,* (1526).
11. See ante, pp.

riage as constant and unchanging as that in which he stands to the human race created by him and the object of his love. 'My covenant will I not break, nor alter the thing that is gone out of my lips.'[12] But in a world of change, and a sinful world, personal relationships change and sometimes they deteriorate, and marriages break down. Marriages, even the marriages of Christians, are not exempt from the conditioning influences of the world and society and the empirical facts of human nature, 'as if some ideal Platonic form of marital union were projected into each couple as they knelt at the altar'.[13] Even penitence and forgiveness may not always avail to restore the marriage relationship, for temperamental and other factors may enter in to make living together impossible.

On this view of marriage - the view that a marriage may 'die' when the personal reality has departed from it - remarriage after divorce becomes permissible, and with it the prospect is opened up of a new life and a new union which with God's blessing may redeem the failure of the first. It is a view which for centuries has been taken by the Eastern Churches, it is the view of the Reformed Churches, including the English Free Churches, and it has been strongly represented in the Church of England itself from the time of the Reformation onwards.

If this view of marriage were to be officially adopted in the Church of England, questions of procedure would still remain to be settled. Not all second marriages could rightly be solemnised with the Church's blessing;[14] and some means of deciding between one case and another would have to be devised. It could be left, as Archdeacon Edward Carpenter recommended,[15] to the discretion of the individual clergyman, but this would undoubtedly lead to too great diversity of practice and to the widespread transgression of parochial boundaries by couples going from parish to parish to find an incumbent willing to marry them. A more satisfactory solution to the problem of procedure would be to follow a course similar to that laid down in the

12. Psalm 89. 34.
13. Edward Carpenter, 'Marriage in the Church of England', *The Modern Churchman,* September 1954, p. 241.
14. It would not be a case of confining permission to remarry to the innocent party. A guilty party may be truly penitent and sincerely intend to enter into a Christian union. It might be desirable to include in the form of service for the marriage of divorced persons a penitential element and a prayer for forgiveness of past failure, as does the form of service used in such cases by the Orthodox Churches.
15. Carpenter, 'Marriage in the Church of England', *The Modern Churchman,* September 1954, p. 251.

1967 Marriage Canon of the Anglican Church of Canada, and to set up in each diocese a body to review all applications for remarriage in church after divorce. Such a body, like the Ecclesiastical Matrimonial Commission in the Canadian dioceses, would before granting or withholding permission take all relevant facts into account, the cause of the marriage breakdown, the efforts made at reconciliation, the prospects of the stability of the intended marriage, and the parties' understanding of the Church's teaching concerning marriage and their intention to enter into a Christian union.

Against this proposal it might be urged that it is open to the same objections as have been brought against the proposal to establish Church Courts to decide possible cases of nullity. There is, however, an answer to this. A nullity tribunal is of necessity juridical, being concerned with highly technical matters of law and fact, and often requiring for its decision evidence concerning events, and even states of mind, in the distant past. A Commission or other body for the consideration of applications for marriage in church after divorce would be primarily a pastoral one, and though the causes of the breakdown of the first marriage would be among the factors to be taken into account, its main concern would be with the present situation, with the intentions and resolves of the applicants, with the promise which the intended marriage holds for the future, and with the possibility of a strong and stable Christian married life resulting from it.[16]

One question remains to be considered in conclusion, and it is bound to trouble those Christians who take what might be called a 'liberal' position in the matter of remarriage after divorce. It is this: are we betraying the sacrifice of those who are determined at all costs to be true to their original vows in spite of their marriage having broken down? What of the husband or wife who says, 'When I married I took my vows to God. No matter what she (or he) has done, those vows stand'?[17] God forbid that anything should be said or implied to belittle such a sacrifice, especially in an age when the desire for an easy and costless Christianity prevents so many Christians from hearing and heeding the call to take up the Cross. But here surely it

16. The Canadian Canon has a nullity procedure, or as it is called, 'the determination of marital status under this Canon', alongside that for the application to remarry in church after divorce. The latter provision, however, would appear to make the former largely unnecessary, except in certain rare cases.
17. A case of this kind is cited by Leonard Hodgson in *Sex and Christian Freedom,* p. 75.

is a case of God's vocation for each individual. There are those who are called to glorify God by entering upon a second marriage after the breakdown of the first and by making it, by his grace, the best that it is in them to make it. There are others who are called to glorify him by renouncing a second union out of fidelity to the vows of the first. The words of Jesus are applicable here: 'Not all men can receive this saying, but they to whom it is given . . . . . . He that is able to receive it let him receive it.'[18]

18. Matthew, 19. 11, 12.

INDEX